Art Nouveau and Art Deco
Lamps and Candlesticks

Wolf Uecker

Art Nouveau and Art Deco
Lamps and Candlesticks

Photographs by Jacques Hartz

Thames and Hudson

First published in Great Britain in 1986 by Thames and Hudson Ltd, London

Printed and bound in Italy

CONTENTS

INTRODUCTION

Since the period at the turn of the century, known in stylistic terms as Jugendstil in Germany and Art Nouveau in France and England, a period praised by our grandfathers, mocked or condemned by our fathers, and only now rediscovered by our own generation, the same questions have repeatedly been asked.

Are the applied arts really art? Is the craftsman an artist or just a man who works with his hands? Can one conceive of the one without the other? These are questions to which the present book, which deals with lamps and candlesticks, can provide no definitive answers. Although every page of illustration shows, through examples in bronze, glass and other materials, that the craftsman must be an artist, and that the artist can also be a craftsman, the definition remains a matter of personal interpretation and sentiment. Symbolical statements, poetic combinations of colour and functional Cubist forms, realized through old or newly discovered techniques, achieve a new artistic significance in the works figured here. In describing this exclusive selection, therefore, we have dispensed with banal terms such as "light fixtures", and instead of talking about "illuminated objects", we refer simply to "lamps and candlesticks".

Thomas Edison's discovery of the incandescent lamp must have seemed like a miracle to people in the 1890s, and the combination of the metal coil with a high-quality glass bulb resulted in a technical revolution. This new technical miracle was soon put to an enormous number of uses, achieving spectacular results in the lighting of houses, towns and public meeting places. In order to understand the effect of this magic gift of sunlight, which changed night into day at the simple pressing of a switch, one must try to imagine the homely evenings of that period, the oppressive twilight filled with the smell of petroleum, or the hiss of pale gaslight, spreading its air of tragedy. Otto Erich Hartleben was still able to write in 1885: "The only acceptable source of light is the candle, everything else is finally only an illuminated smell."

Hardly had Edison's invention been perfected

for industrial purposes than a wealth of new lamps were being created to accommodate the new source of light. Electric light was lovingly surrounded with bouquets of glass flowers; it shone with an exotic gleam through fruits, flowers and leaves of transparent glass, and crowned, as a naked light bulb, bronze sculptures and fanciful decorations of intricate craftsmanship. Those who believed in progress were eager to see it demonstrated.

One of the greatest problems in the history of mankind, that of precise lighting, was solved by electricity during this period. All other sources of illumination up until then had not been able to give any, or only little, concentrated light. Electricity, on the other hand, could be adapted without difficulty to any design, shape or line that an artistic imagination might invent. Tiffany wrote: "Lamplight should conjure up the day's sun-filled hours at any time."

The period we shall be dealing with in this book, 1890 to 1930, was influenced by two artistic styles: Jugendstil, which finally returned to favour after the epoch-making exhibition at the Zurich Museum in 1952, and Art Deco, which took its impulse from the Bauhaus, the industrial designers' studios, and the interior designers and artists of the twenties. The revival of Art Deco followed years of neglect (or contempt) and it was not until the big Paris exposition "Les Années Vingt-Cinq" in 1966 that the interest of the public at large was re-awakened.

The choice of objects represented here is necessarily subjective because of the very number of the artists and manufacturers concerned and of the objects of quality which they produced. Our yardstick has not been the fashion for "nostalgia", which has flooded the market with imitations of lamps and candlesticks, nor the current value of items on the art scene, but rather the maxim used by Samuel Bing to define the objectives of his new gallery, L'Art Nouveau, opened on 1 October 1895: "All works of art shall be admitted which show a personal independence and are in harmony with the spirit of the age."

Since this book is intended not only to inspire the keen collector, and inform the art dealer, but also to make the subject clear to anyone else who may be interested in it, we should add that Bing's objective can only be partially achieved here. So much is still to be discovered. Art historians are only now beginning systematically to sort and evaluate. Being myself an avid collector, I write this with the reader in mind who may miss something here which he or she loves, or find it only mentioned in passing. My co-author and friend Jacques Hartz, who is also a collector, has received willing support and valuable recommendations for his photographic work from museums and collections in Europe and the USA. There is one regrettable exception: due to lack of co-operation from the Musée de l'Ecole de Nancy, we have been unable to include any of the works from that museum's collection. The decision to deal with lamps and candlesticks in one volume was not an easy one, but it seemed appropriate to document the total production of each manufacturer and artist, rather than to split up the results of my research into two volumes. For the same reason, it was decided against separating the colour from the black and white photographs.

My Parisian friends Madame Luce Morel and the painter and collector Barlach Heuer have sacrificed a great deal of time in research and given much informed advice towards the promoting and completion of this book.

To Lillian Nassau in New York I owe my very special thanks. Without her guidance in this subject over many years, the beauty of lamps and candlesticks might have passed me by.

I AUSTRIA

Gustav Gurschner

Born in Mühldorf, Bavaria, in 1873. Sculptor in Vienna. Date of death unknown.

Studied in Bozen and at the School of Arts and Crafts in Vienna, as well as in Paris (1887), which particularly influenced him and where some of his works were bought by the Musée Galliera.

In 1898 he took part in the opening of the Wiener Secession, providing work in the applied arts field.

He contributed to many exhibitions of arts and crafts and received commissions from all over the world. Gurschner created portraits, monuments, medals and, above all, small figures and novel lamps.

What fascinated him most was the task of finding a pleasing aesthetic solution, different from the usual type of illumination, for this new kind of light.

1 *Decorative lamp*
Base and stem of bronze.
A female figure embraces a tree which surrounds a nautilus shell made out of Bohemian art glass.
~ 1905
Sign. Gurschner
H: 45 cm

2 *Table-lamp*
Nautilus shell, in a figurative white-metal setting, representing a girl.
~ 1900
Gurschner (?)
H: 33 cm ⌀: Shell 13 cm

3 *Candlestick*
For use with either light bulb or candle. Patinated bronze.
~ 1899
Sign. Gurschner
Ill. *The Artist*, (London, 1900), p. 77

4 *Table-lamp*
Nautilus shell, held by a female figure. Bronze.
~ 1900
Sign. Gustav Gurschner
H: 54 cm ⌀: 16 cm

7   Small lamp
Nautilus shell with a fine pewter
mount; can be used either as a
hanging lamp or table-lamp.
Abstract floral pattern.
~ 1900
Attributed to: Gustav Gurschner
H: 26 cm

8   Table-lamp
Two stylized bronze trees
supporting the lustre-glass
domes.
~ 1900
Sign. Gurschner
H: 40 cm

5   Table-lamp
Golden yellow lustre glass with
silver-blue *Candia Silver Iris*
overlay, and decorated with blue
glass threads. The bronze base
has a brown patina, with stylized
silver buds on the shade support.
~ 1900
Shade: Joh. Loetz Witwe
Base: Sign. Gurschner Deposé
H: 39.5 cm   Ø: 25 cm

6   Candlestick
Bronze figure.
December 1900 Sign. Gustav
Gurschner, Vienna
H: 27 cm

Carl Hagenauer

Born in 1872, died in 1928. Engraver and master caster, who founded the Hagenauer workshop in 1898. His oldest son Karl, born in 1898, was a pupil of Josef Hoffmann. After 1919, Karl worked in his father's workshop, his style influenced by the Wiener Werkstätte in the search for a modern form expressive of the twenties.
The architect Julius Jirasek joined him in 1930 in his efforts to apply Neue Sachlichkeit principles to all areas of the applied arts. Karl's brother Franz Hagenauer, born in 1906, completed the trio.
He became Professor at the Academy of Applied Arts in Vienna in 1962.

9   *Table-lamp*
Base and shaft in alpaca. Stylized figure of a female dancer surrounded by animals.
Cloth shade.
Manufacture: Karl Hagenauer
Sign. WHW 1926
Marked: Made in Austria
H: 43 cm

10   *Table-lamp*
Base and sculpture in alpaca, representing a man with a dog.
Stretched cloth shade.
Manufacture: Karl Hagenauer
Sign. WHW 1926
H: 54 cm

Josef Hoffmann

Born in Pirnitz near Iglau, Mähren, in 1870, died in Vienna in 1956.

Architect and fine arts and graphic designer. Studied at the Vienna Academy under Otto Wagner. Was a founder member of the Wiener Secession in 1897. Two years later he became Professor of Architecture at the Vienna School of Arts and Crafts. In 1903, together with Koloman Moser and Fritz Wärndorfer, he founded the Wiener Werkstätte and he assumed artistic direction there until 1931. As initiator and director of the Österreichischer Werkbund he had, through his own work, a dominant influence on architecture, all branches of the fine arts, and even film and theatre productions in Austria.

11   *Decorative lamp*
Beaten brass, handmade.
Sign. J. Hoffmann, Wiener
Werkstätte
H: 34 cm

12   *Table-lamp*
White silk shade with black
trimmings on a brass base.
Sign. Josef Hoffmann,
J. H. Wiener Werkstätte
H: 31 cm   Ø: 14 cm

Johann Loetz Witwe

Situated at Klostermühle, near Unterreichenstein, West Bohemia, these works consisted of blown-glass furnaces and refineries for ornamental and utility glassware, lighting elements, wall coverings and windows. They were suppliers of crude glass to L. C. Tiffany, New York. Founded in 1836 by Johann B. Eisner, they were bought in 1840 by Johann Loetz (1778-1848), after whose death the works went under the name Johann Loetz Witwe.

In 1879 the furnaces were taken over by Loetz's grandson, Max Ritter von Spaun, and he modernized the works.

In 1887 a patent was taken out on the production of multicoloured glass, and, in 1898, on the application of lustre techniques. As early as the 1880s and 1890s the works were producing iridescent glass and glass with multicoloured inlay.

In Paris in 1899 the firm showed their first *Papillongläser*, glass with shiny iridescent spots, and *Phänomengläser*, glass with inlayed and overlayed combed glass threads, partly metal-coloured, similar to Tiffany glass.

In 1900, at the World Exhibition in Paris, Loetz was awarded the Grand Prix. The firm was at this time one of the most important glassworks in Europe. After 1902 the firm attracted designers like Maria Kirschner of Berlin and leading artists of the Wiener Werkstätte, among them Josef Hoffmann, Dagobert Peche, Michael Powolny, Otto Prutscher, and Koloman Moser and his pupils.

Max Ritter von Spaun died in 1909. The glassworks carried on under the direction of Adolf Beckert, and produced cased glass in the style of the French Art Nouveau.

The last time Loetz exhibited was at the applied arts exhibition in Paris in 1925, with a collection of glass decorated with thread inlay and lustre effects, designed by, among others, Prutscher.

13 *Hanging lamp*
Brass. The flex is spread apart by a brass ring. On each cord are two glass balls; the brass ring is decorated with jewelled glass. The five opaline globes are decorated in a feather pattern with applied blue drops.
~ 1900
H: 100 cm   Ø: 12 cm (globe)

14 *Hanging lamp*
Inverted dome shape with six globes. Hand-beaten brass frame. The glass parts have a *Papillon* design with lava glass areas.
~ 1900
H: 102 cm   Ø: 87 cm

15 Table-lamp
Orange-coloured lustre glass
with green wave-pattern, on a
pewter base.
~ 1900
Sign. Loetz
H: 57.5 cm   Ø: 17.5 cm
Lit. Victor Arwas, *Glass Art
Nouveau to Art Deco,* p. 145

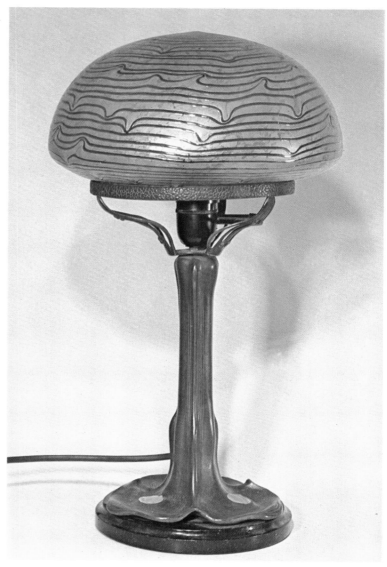

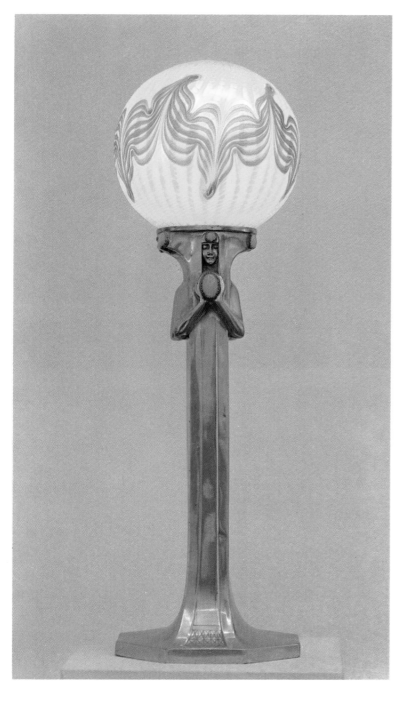

16 Table-lamp
Violet, gold and blue iridescent
lustre glass, with a green glass
thread running spirally over the
shade's surface. Bronze base with
mother-of-pearl inlay in a
satinflower shape, and floral
design, mounted on a wooden
stand.
~ 1898
H: 46 cm   Ø: 17.5 cm

17 Pair of candlesticks
Yellow-green *Papillon* lustre
glass, with melted glass threads.
The shaft is twisted to the right in
the manner of a corkscrew.
~ 1900
H: 14 cm

18 Table-lamp
The onion-shaped Loetz-glass
dome rests on a silver base, and
the glass has a silvery gold
Papillon design with a border of
blue glass threads laid close
together.
~ 1900
H: 34 cm

20 Decorative lamp
The bronze figure stands on a
marble base and carries an
onion-shaped bulb made of Loetz
glass. The shade is made of
honey-coloured opaline with
blue-green threads.
Bronze sign. G. de Keruéguen
H: 64 cm

21 Table-lamp
Base and shaft of patinated
bronze. Three women dance in a
circle around the stem. The
shade is of striped opaline with
Papillon decoration, overlaid
with yellow, pink and red. Glass:
Loetz Wtw.
Bronze sign. Pohl
H: 55 cm

19 Floor-lamp
Base consisting of female figure
made of coloured terracotta.
Dome of golden yellow iridescent
glass with *Papillon* design.
Signature indecipherable.
Scratched on the base is:
"Weng + Lengsfeld, Köln-
Lindenthal"
H: 100 cm   ∅: 22 cm

22   *Table-lamp*
The orange-coloured lustre-glass
dome is supported by a wrought-
iron base with floral decorations.
H: 51 cm   Ø: 14 cm

23   *Table-lamp*
Mushroom-shaped lamp, made
of lustre glass and decorated with
a blue *Iris-Papillon* design and
silver spots. Base of moulded
lustre glass. Setting of polished
bronze.
1906/1910
Manufacturer: Wiener
Werkstätte (?)
Extremely rare
H: 74.5 cm   Ø: 40 cm

24 Table-lamp
The base is made of lustre glass striped with threads of iridescent silver and orange and held, top and bottom, by a silver-gilt mount. The mount depicts four dolphins diving into waves. The shade is covered with watered silk. The lamp was specially produced for the Tsar Nicholas for use on his luxury yacht. The frame bears the signature *Fabergé and the initials of the master craftsman, Johan Victor Aarne.
H: 22.5 cm

*Fabergé, Peter Carl
Born in St Petersburg in 1846, died in Lausanne in 1920. Court goldsmith and jeweller to the Russian Emperor.
Son of the Protestant goldsmith Gustav Fabergé (1814-93), who was born in Pernau, Lithuania, of a family of probable Huguenot descent. The end of the Revolution saw the closing of the firm in 1918 and Fabergé's subsequent flight to Switzerland via Riga, Berlin, Frankfurt and Hamburg. He was a member of the jury at the Paris World Exhibition, became a master craftsman and was awarded the Cross of the Legion of Honour.

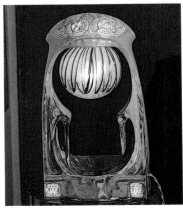

25 Table-lamp
Base and frame for the dome made of coloured faïence decorated with an abstract design. Produced by Bieler of Bohemia, after a design by Dressler. The coloured glass sphere is overlaid with threads and a *Papillon* design by Loetz Wtw.
~ 1900
H: 39 cm

Emanuel Josef Margold

Born in Vienna in 1889, died in Bratislava in 1962. After training as a cabinet-maker at the Technical School of Woodwork in Königsberg on the Eger, he became a pupil of Anton Huber at the School of Arts and Crafts in Mainz and then studied architecture at the Academy in Vienna under Josef Hoffmann.
Between 1908 and 1909 he undertook various building commissions in Czechoslovakia and Austria and worked as assistant to Hoffmann at the Academy and at the latter's studio at the Wiener Werkstätte. In 1911 he was invited to join the Artists' Colony in Darmstadt where he produced a number of designs for furniture, wallpaper, glass and porcelain objects and, in 1914, designed exhibition halls for the Colony. In 1929 he left Darmstadt and settled in Berlin.

26 Table-lamp
Beaten-brass base. Silk shade.
1914
H: 46 cm   W: 18.5 cm
⌀: 20 cm

Rudolf Ferdinand Marschall

Born in Vienna in 1873, date of death unknown. A medallist, he studied at the School of Engravers and, from 1896 to 1898, under Tautenhayn at the Academy of Decorative Arts in Vienna. From 1905 to 1938 he was Director of the Vienna School of Engravers and Medallists.

27 *Table-lamp*
Base and shaft are of brass. A female figure holds the cloth-covered lampshade.
~ 1914
Sign. Prof. Rudolf Marschall
H: 34 cm

Dagobert Peche

Born in Salzburg in 1887, died in Vienna in 1923, aged thirty-six. The son of a notary, he attended secondary school, studied at the Academy in Vienna, and was awarded the Prix de Rome. In 1911 he spent six month in Paris where he designed his first armchair, the Louvre Chair (Lit.: Max Eisler, *Dagobert Peche*, 1925).

The year 1913 saw the appearance of his first illustrated cycle, *Liebe und Tanz* (Darmstädter Monatshefte). His fabric designs were executed by Backhausen & Sons, his wallpaper designs by Max Schmidt and his furniture designs by the cabinet-maker Soulek, all in Vienna. In 1915, Peche joined the Wiener Werkstätte where he headed an "artists' workshop".

Up until the 1920s his ideas and designs influenced many artists at the Wiener Werkstätte, in particular Josef Hoffmann. He contributed designs for a fashion show at the Museum of Applied Arts in Vienna.

He took over the directorship of the Zurich branch of the Wiener Werkstätte in 1917 and his designs for the interior decorations of the premises marked a high point in his artistic career.

In 1921 he designed a series of wallpapers for the firms of Flammerstein & Steinmann in Cologne and Max Schmidt in Vienna, and fabrics for the Backhausen firm in Vienna. In Vienna, from 1919 to 1923, he produced numerous sketches and finished drawings for furniture, lamps, chandeliers, pots and jewellery which were executed by the Wiener Werkstätte and the ceramics manufacturer Schleiss in Gmunden.

28 *Hanging lamp*
Brass, with nine lights. Both dish and globe are made of milk glass.
~ 1918
Sign. Dagobert Peche
H: 112 cm

29 *Hanging lamp*
The brass rods are decorated with abstract designs; hollow ribbed glass rods are suspended from the nine lights.
~ 1918
Dagobert Peche (?)
H: 110 cm   Ø: 110 cm

30 *Table-lamp*
The ceramic base with abstract
decoration supports a yellow
cloth shade with a tiny dome.
Wiener Werkstätte.
Attributed to: Dagobert Peche
H: 86 cm

31 *Candelabrum*
Three polished-bronze arms;
stylized female figure on a broad
base.
~ 1920
(Attributed to the Dagobert Peche
workshop at the Wiener
Werkstätte.)
H: 40 cm

Wiener Werkstätte

Founded in 1903, with Josef Hoffmann and
Koloman Moser (1868-1918) as artistic directors.
The programme of the Wiener Werkstätte was
first published in 1905. It is clear from the latter
that the workshops were working at this time
exclusively from the designs of the two artistic
directors. The objective of the workshops was
not only to produce individual *objets d'art*, but
also to design complete interiors and to build
houses. Their productions set the new style in
Vienna. Among the leading members were: C. O.
Czeschka, Michael Powolny and Gustav Klimt.
Geometric form and decor, the main feature of
the early period, derived from the designs of the
Scottish couple C. R. Mackintosh and Margaret
Macdonald, and of C. R. Ashbee.
Eduard Josef Wimmer became a member in
1908 and applied himself chiefly to fashion. From
1915, Dagobert Peche gave the workshops a new,
more decorative direction. The Wiener
Werkstätte achieved a further high point in the
1920s with the production of embroidery, lace
and needlework, creating in this area a personal
style which was to remain their hallmark for the
next twenty years.

32 *Table-lamp*
The decorated brass base and
shaft support a fabric lampshade.
~ 1923
Sign. Wiener Werkstätte,
Dagobert Peche
H: 79 cm

Vilmos Zsolnay

Born and died in Pécs, Hungary (1828-1900).
A ceramist, in 1865 he took over his brother's
ceramics firm in Pécs (Fünfkirchen) and by
increasing its artistic and technical range turned
it into a thriving concern. In 1874 he achieved his
first great success at the World Exhibition in
Vienna. His speciality lay in the production of
various kinds of enamels.

During the course of his work with the chemist
V. Wartha (from 1892) Zsolnay discovered the
ruby-red glaze known as "Eosin". The firm's
distributor in Vienna was Wahliss.

In 1899, Zsolnay's son, Miklos, took over the
direction of the firm, which began producing
works in the Art Nouveau style, including
statuettes, animal figurines, lamps with
figurative decorations, and vases. Among the
designers working for the firm at this time were
Josef Rippl-Ronay and Laszlo von
Mattyasovszky.

Between 1900 and 1915, Zsolnay developed the
production of building blocks and tiles. During
the Second World War, production was limited
almost entirely to industrial goods and high
tension insulators.

In 1949 the firm was nationalized and became
Porzelangyar Pécs.

Since the 1950s it has brought out reproductions
of statuettes and vases from old models, though
of inferior quality.

33 *Decorative lamp*
A female figure in lustre faïence
holds the shade above her head.
~ 1900
Stamped: Zsolnay Pécs
H: 58 cm

34 *Decorative lamp*
Faïence with lustre glaze,
representing a squatting satyr
carrying a mussel shell which
conceals the light bulb.
~ 1910
Sign. A B T Sandor No. 8280
H: 32 cm

35 *Decorative lamp*
Porcelain-faïence (partly lustre
glazed), representing a reclining
satyr. The entire lamp is covered
with gold-green lustre.
~ 1901
Sign. Mack Lajos No. 6236
H: 26 cm

36 *Candlestick*
Ceramic, with a rich blue-green
lustre glaze.
~ 1905
Sign. Zsolnay, Pécs
H: 13 cm

No closer identification

37 *Hanging lamp*
Bars and canopy of embossed
brass, five lights, in the centre a
milk-glass dome. Square border
of hollow glass rods.
~ 1905
Possibly Koloman Moser
H: 130 cm   Ø: 55 cm

40 *Decorative lamp*
Nude figure of a girl, surrounded
by leaves which swirl up to form a
wreath of flowers. Cast and
patinated bronze.
~ 1900
H: 47 cm

38 *Hanging lamp*
Canopy and ring of engraved
brass. Six milk-glass globes are
suspended from cords decorated
with large glass balls.
~ 1914
H: 137 cm   Ø: 70 cm

41 *Table-lamp*
Base and lamp of polished
bronze, representing a goose-
girl, whose face is made of ivory.
The lampshade is set with five
glass stones.
~ 1900
Sign. P. Tereszezuk
H: 33 cm

39 *Table-lamp*
Base of burnished brass in the
form of branches, decorated with
white glass pearls. Clear drapery-
glass shade overlaid with close-
knit branches and leaves.
~ 1900
H: 44.7 cm

42 *Small lamp*
Silvered-pewter, female figure
holding a flower, on a broad base.
~ 1900
Austria, stamped with double
eagle and crown, and also
bearing the monogram M. H.
H: 32.5 cm

44 *Candlestick*
Silver and green enamel.
Vienna 1899. Firm Gg. Adam
Scheidt.
H: 22.5 cm

43 *Pair of candlesticks*
Bronze, male and female nudes.
Sign. E. K., and marked
Kunsterzgiesserei Wien 1296 und
1298
H: 9 cm   W: 12.5 cm

II BELGIUM

Victor Horta

Belgian architect and designer (1861-1947). A pioneer of the Art Nouveau style, he achieved harmonious effects in his designs for furniture and interiors by the careful selection of types of wood, colour of door frames, wall panelling, etc. Characteristic of Victor Horta's work are his simple forms, striking lines and use of stylized flower designs. Horta designed furniture and interiors for the Hôtel Solvay and the famous Maison Tassel in Brussels.

His architectural work, door mounts, lamps and candlesticks, all bear the unmistakable mark of his style.

45 *Candelabrum*
Silvered metal, with five arms.
Design by Victor Horta. Exhib.
Turin 1902.
~ 1898
Sign. Fernand Dubois
H: 56 cm   Ø: 42 cm

46 *Candelabrum*
Patinated bronze, with five arms.
Design by Victor Horta
Marked in bronze:
Kunstgiesserei Brüssel
H: 48.5 cm   W: 35.5 cm

Henry Clemens van de Velde

Born in Antwerp in 1863, died in Zurich in 1957. painter, architect, designer of interiors and *objets d'art*. He studied painting in Antwerp (1881-83) and Paris (1884-85), and later in Brussels. Under the influence of William Morris he switched in 1890 to architecture and the applied arts. From 1893 to 1894 he gave a course of lectures at the Academy in Antwerp. In 1895 he drew up the plans for his own house in Uccle near Brussels. During the years 1889-1902 he designed the Folkwang Museum in Hagen. He travelled in Germany during 1897 and 1898 and in 1900 moved to Berlin. From 1902 he was artistic adviser to the Grand Duke Wilhelm Ernst in Weimar. In 1903 he undertook a voyage to the Orient. From 1906 to 1914 he directed the School of Arts and Crafts in Weimar. In 1907 he became a founder member of the Deutscher Werkbund. In 1914 he designed the Deutscher Werkbund Exhibition in Cologne. In 1925 he received a commission to found the Institut Supérieur d'Architecture et des Arts Décoratifs in Belgium. In 1937 and 1939-40 he designed the Belgian Pavilion at the World Exhibition. From 1947 until his death van de Velde lived in Switzerland. In 1958 a Memorial Exhibition was set up in his honour in the Museum of Applied Arts in Zurich.

47 *Pair of candlesticks*
Silver, with two branches, abstract decoration and round base. Bears the signature of Henry van de Velde. Th. Müller, registered, German silver Mark, moon and crown, 800. Numbered 1157, 1158. See catalogue *H. van de Velde*, Galérie L'Ecuyer (Brussels, 1970), p. 88, Ill. No. 171a.
1905 Weimar
H: 26 cm

48 *Candlestick*
Silvered bronze, with two branches.
1902 Weimar
H: 27.5 cm
Ill. Hammacher, *Le Monde de Henry van de Velde*, p. 121

Franz Hoosemans, Egide Rombeaux

Hoosemans and Rombeaux, both from Brussels, worked in silver and ivory. Rombeaux was born in 1865.

49 *Candlestick*
Three-branched silver candlestick, representing stylized thistle stems with a floating female figure in ivory. This object, together with a pendant, was bought by the Berlin Museums at the Paris World Exhibition in 1900 for 2,200 Goldmark.
A similar piece has been stolen from the Museum für Kunst und Gewerbe, Hamburg.
H: 36 cm

50 *Candle holder*
With inkpot and two receptacles left and right. Also has a lid.
Sign. A. Jef. Strymans
H: 13 cm   W: 27 cm

III FRANCE

Gabriel Argy-Rousseau

Born in Meslay-le-Vidome in 1885. He began his artistic career as a ceramist, glassmaker and designer in 1906 and embraced in turn both the Art Nouveau and the Art Deco styles. Although he had earlier achieved worldwide fame, Argy-Rousseau died in obscurity at the age of sixty-eight and never lived to see his comeback. Joseph Gabriel Rousseau, who chose the pseudonym Gabriel Argy-Rousseau in 1914, came from a working-class country family. An outstanding pupil, he was granted a scholarship for further education. Apart from a talent for physics and chemistry he showed a strong inclination for art. He was accepted in 1902 at the Ecole Nationale de Céramique in Sèvres. One of his contemporaries was Jean Cros, whose father Henri rediscovered the *pâte-de-verre* technique. It is very probable that Argy-Rousseau got to know his colleague's father at that time, as his workshop was in a former building of the Sèvres firm. This would also explain the marked interest which Argy-Rousseau already showed for *pâte-de-verre* during that period. He passed his final examination with distinction. Immediately afterwards he received the directorship of an experimental ceramics laboratory, and a little later he equipped his own workshop in Paris for the production of *pâte-de-verre* and *pâte-de-cristal*.

In 1914 he exhibited his first art-glass objects, which were still very much influenced by the floral Art Nouveau style. The war interrupted his work. After 1918 he began to exploit the various structural possibilities offered by his favourite material. His work tended increasingly towards a geometrical style and after 1922 he was an enthusiastic exponent of Art Deco. He soon became well known and took part in all the major exhibitions. In 1921 he founded, without any previous business experience, a joint-stock company under the name "Les Pâtes de Verres d'Argy-Rousseau". This firm employed a few dozen craftsmen. At the great exposition of arts and crafts in Paris in 1925, which gave the Art Deco style its name, he was a member of the committee which judged the glass section. His creations, now known in France and throughout the world, were much in demand. The worldwide economic crisis of 1929 first hit the market for luxury goods and Argy-Rousseau was forced to close his studios in 1930. He continued to create a few pieces, which are valued today at very high prices, but his creative powers slowly waned and, although he still exhibited in Paris up until the fifties, Argy-Rousseau produced and sold nothing new, living off his savings. He died in 1953.

Only recently has anything come to light about Argy-Rousseau's life history and technical methods. Whereas other artists like Almaric Walter and Cros shaped their objects using the *cire-perdue* method, Argy-Rousseau made his models out of a number of pieces of plaster that fitted one into another. Over this first model hot wax was carefully poured and provided the mould for the second layer of plaster which would give the object its definitive form. The glass was special pulverized glass, variously coloured by the addition of metal oxides and mixed with water to form a paste. After a number of other processes, the glass paste was pressed into the mould in several layers each about four millimetres thick. This process, simplified in our description, ended with the mould being placed in the oven and slowly baked, like a cake, at a low temperature. After cooling off, the object was freed from the mould and carefully cleaned. Argy-Rousseau's many lamps, both large and small, were all made by this method.

51 *Table-lamp*
Pâte-de-verre, on a hammered
wrought-iron base. The
illuminated body has a frieze of
antique masks, above which runs
an abstract circular decoration
which is repeated on the shade.
~ 1915
Sign. Argy-Rousseau
H: 40 cm   Ø: 21 cm

52 Table-lamp
Bronze base; four arms support
the *pâte-de-verre* dome which is
deep purple, blending into dark
green at the top, and decorated
with a pattern of stylized leaves.
Sign. Argy-Rousseau
H: 35 cm   Ø: 15 cm

53 *Small lamp*
Pâte-de-verre, on a hammered,
wrought-iron stand, with
rounded feet. Brown-beige,
tinged with violet and green, and
decorated with red antique
masks.
~ 1915
Sign. Argy-Rousseau
H: 12 cm   Ø: 8 cm
Ill. *Le Style* (1925), p. 183

54 Table-lamp
Hammered cast-iron base with a
mount reaching up around the
body. *Pâte-de verre* shade with
abstract Art Deco design.
Colours: lilac, dark blue, red and
light green.
~ 1925
Sign. Argy-Rousseau
H: 40 cm   Ø: 19 cm

55 Small table-lamp
Dark blue, red and purple *pâte-
de-verre*, with a decoration of
stylized flowers. The base is
hammered wrought iron.
~ 1914
Edgar Brandt (?)
Sign. Argy-Rousseau
H: 39 cm

56 Small lamp
Base of hammered wrought iron.
(Sign. Van Lov.) *Pâte-de-verre*
shade with geometrical Art Deco
motif. Colours: red, brown, blue,
lilac.
~ 1920
Sign. Argy-Rousseau
H: 30 cm   Ø: 7 cm

Maurice Barret

Nothing further is known of Barret than that he was born in Besançon, worked as an interior designer and, as an old man, exhibited a childrens' library at the Salon d'Automne in 1936.

57 *Desk-lamp*
The moveable lampshade, mounted on a wooden base, has chrome counterweights. The shade is made of lacquered steel plate.
~ 1929
H: 90 cm   Ø: 13 cm

Maurice Bouval

Born in Toulouse, died in Paris, around 1920. A pupil of Falguière, he quickly achieved recognition as a sculptor. He rarely produced lamps or candlesticks; the few sought-after pieces that do exist are mostly floral sculptures in bronze. When he designed a shade for the light bulb it was usually of *pâte-de-verre*, made by the manufacturers Daum Frères* of Nancy, and represented a bud or an illuminated flower. He was a member of the Société des Artistes Français and was frequently commended for his work, as, for example, at the 1900 World Exhibition in Paris.

*now known as the Cristalleries de Nancy

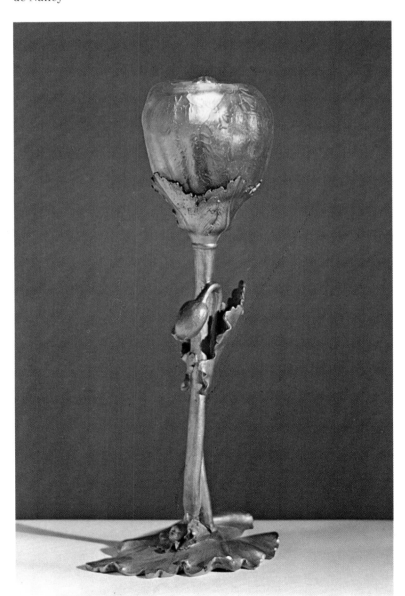

58 *Decorative lamp*
The gilded-bronze base and stem depict the poppy leaf and bud and support a colourless *pâte-de-verre* dome.
~ 1898
Sign. Bouval
H: 32 cm

59 *Decorative lamp*
A bronze sculpture depicting a thistle with bud and leaves; the flower is in *pâte-de-verre* by Daum Frères of Nancy.
~ 1900
The sculpture is signed underneath: M. Bouval.
Compare: *Le Modern Style*, p. 173, Ill. No. 8
H: 53 cm

60   *Pair of candlesticks*
Gilded bronze. Marked "Rêverie et ...(illegible)".
~ 1900
Sign. Bouval
H: 45.5 cm

Edgar Brandt

Born in Paris in 1880, died in 1960. He called himself an "art smith" and, even before 1920, was successfully combining in his designs two completely opposite materials: glass and iron. A Parisian of Alsatian background, Brandt received his education in Paris and made a name for himself early on with his unusual designs for grates, lamps, mirror frames and a new kind of chandelier. He was a member of the Société des Arts Décoratifs, the Artistes Français and the Salon d'Automne.

In Paris, around 1925, he was the only craftsman to be working with wrought metal and was represented at the 1925 Exhibition, "Arts Décoratifs et Industriels Modernes". His creations brought a cool, new dimension to the often dismal or all too colourful, overfilled rooms: the precision of gilded, silvered and patinated metals. Brandt collaborated in the

creation of his metal and glass designs with manufacturers like Daum Frères of Nancy and Sabino of Paris, among others. See also Documentation.

61   *Table-lamp*
The wrought-iron base, richly decorated with leaves and flowers, supports a moulded *pâte-de-verre* lampshade.
~ 1925
Base signed E. Brandt. Shade signed Daum/Nancy
H: 47 cm   Ø: 23 cm

62 *Wall-bracket*
These wall-brackets were made
in pairs. Wrought-iron frame
with a decoration of roses; matt
white, acid-etched glass shade.
~ 1925
Sign. E. Brandt
H: 52 cm   W: 60 cm
Ill. *Art Deco*, Octopus Books, p. 44;
Collectors' Encyclopedia, p. 50

63 *Table-lamp*
Wrought-iron base engraved
with geometric motifs; has a
flower-like fixture for the cased-
glass shade which is made of gold
and multicoloured glass with a
reddish overlay.
The glass comes from Daum of
Nancy. The base is signed E.
Brandt.
H: 51 cm   Ø: 35 cm

64 *Table-lamp*
With a geometrical decoration
and a wrought-iron foot on a
round base. The dome is cased
glass with coloured striations.
~ 1925
Base signed E. Brandt. Glass
signed Daum/Nancy
H: 50 cm   Ø: 80 cm

65 *Table-lamp*
Wrought-iron base with stylized
tree motif; alabaster shade held
by a richly decorated finial.
~ 1924
Sign. E. Brandt
H: 48 cm   Ø: 25 cm

66 *Floor-lamp*
Slim wrought-iron stem on a round foot with a filigree-type decoration which continues around the lampshade. Funnel-shaped shade by Daum, made of glass coloured with powder.
~ 1925
Sign. E. Brandt
H: 176 cm   Ø: 36 cm

67 *Hanging lamp*
Wrought-iron frame; five ovoid red and yellow glass shades, four of which form a circle and the fifth, at the centre, hangs lower. The glass has been coloured by the incorporation of melted powder. The body of the lamp is signed E. Brandt; the glass shades are signed Daum/Nancy.
H: 100 cm   Ø: 56 cm

68 *Hanging lamp*
Wrought-iron lamp frame, richly decorated with flowers, with four glass shades made of red and yellow *pâte-de-verre*.
~ 1920

The lamp frame is signed E. Brandt; the shades are signed Daum/Nancy
H: 74 cm   Ø: 34 cm

Albert Cheuret

The life of this artist, like that of many of his contemporaries, has not been well documented. A sculptor and pupil of Perrin and Lemaire, he made his first appearance in 1907 as a member of the Société des Artistes Français.

He designed and constructed the interior and exterior of a shop for the Paris exhibition "Arts Décoratifs et Industriels Modernes" in 1925. The Musée des Arts Décoratifs mentions him in its 1976 catalogue celebrating the Fiftieth Anniversary of that exhibition.

See also Documentation.

69   *Decorative lamp*
The bronze base represents tulip leaves; the illuminated blooms are made of alabaster.
~ 1907
Sign. Albert Cheuret
H: 37 cm

Edward Colonna

Born near Cologne in 1862, died on the French Riviera in 1948. Colonna studied architecture in Brussels and in 1882 emigrated to the United States.

He spent some time in New York working with the group known as "Associated Artists", whose leader was Louis C. Tiffany. He later designed dining cars and sleepers for a firm in Ohio. In 1898 he returned to Paris, where his creative work began in earnest. In collaboration with Samuel Bing's Maison de l'Art Nouveau, he designed furniture, lamp bases, candlesticks, porcelain, fabrics and jewellery, all of which are notable for their graceful shapes and fine lines.

Only a few pieces produced by Colonna in collaboration with other great artists, such as Gallé, are known today. The table-lamp illustrated here and called by Gallé *La Bourrasque* (The Gust of Wind) is a superb example of how two artists can work together, combining complementary skills to produce a homogeneous work of art. After the closure of Bing's gallery, Colonna travelled through Europe and went back once more to New York, where he worked as art dealer and interior designer. He returned to France in 1923 and remained there till his death.

70 *Table-lamp*
La Bourrasque (The Gust of Wind). Cased glass with leaf and mushroom motifs, incorporating *marqueterie de verre*, a colouring of cobalt blue oxide, and a "sandwich" of acid-etched and polished gold leaf. The shade is signed with the Gallé cutting wheel. The bronze base ends in a design of leaves and bears Colonna's signature. The lamp was created by Gallé and Colonna for Samuel Bing's Maison de l'Art Nouveau in Paris in 1898. It is probably unique.
H: 46.5 cm

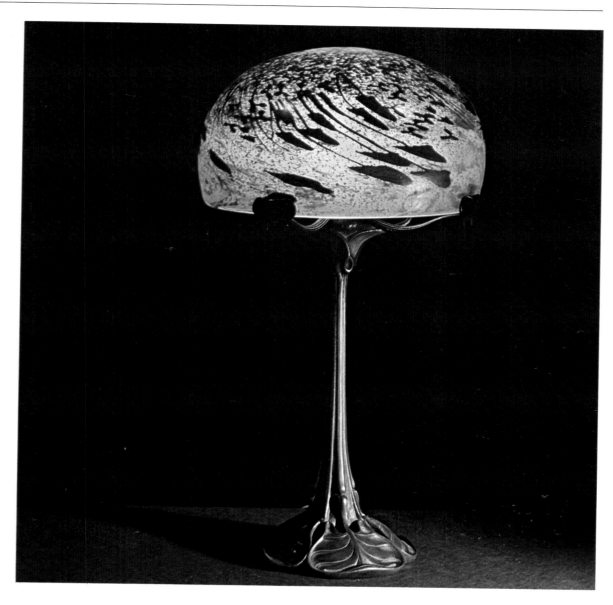

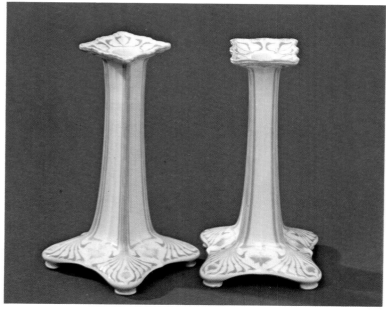

73 *Pair of candlesticks*
Pale green and pink, with an underglaze decoration of flowers. Each candlestick bears the mark of Leuconide (as a guarantee of the porcelain). Signed Colonna and monogrammed ABN (Samuel Bing's Maison de l'Art Nouveau).
H: 24 cm

Aristide-Michel Colotte

Born in Baccarat (1885-1959). He was a member of the Salon des Artistes Français and the Salon d'Automne. He exhibited five crystal vases there in 1928.

72   *Decorative lamp*
Cut crystal, on a rosewood base.
~ 1925
Sign. Colotte, pièce unique
H: 24 cm   W: 50.5 cm

H.A. Copillet & Cie.

Manufacturers of ceramics and glass, both for decorative and functional purposes.
Directed by Henri A. Copillet. From the 1890s the firm produced glass with metallic overlays, often in floral designs. Both A. Duc de Caranza and M. Neuville are known to have worked there. The factory was totally destroyed during the First World War.

73   *Ceiling-light*
Wrought-iron frame, star-shaped canopy.
~ 1900
Marked: Copillet et Cie; glass sign. A. de Caranza (Silzer catalogue, no. 195)
∅: 39 cm

Henri Cros

Lived from 1840 to 1907. His contempories called him "the Man of *Pâte-de-Verre*". Indeed it was he who, around 1884, rediscovered this technique for making glass, which was known to the Egyptians and the Greeks at the time of Pliny. With the help of this versatile technique, Cros executed a whole series of multicoloured statues in *pâte-de-verre*. In 1892 the Manufacture de Sèvres gave him his own studio to use. There he produced his enormous (up to 243 cm long) glass reliefs such as *The History of Water* (1894) and *The History of Fire*, which won him a gold medal at the World Exhibition in Paris in 1900. Cros understood better than almost anyone how to combine the purity of ancient art with the symbolism of Art Nouveau. A few of his wall-brackets are known to us today. His most famous pupil was Georges Despret (1862-1952).

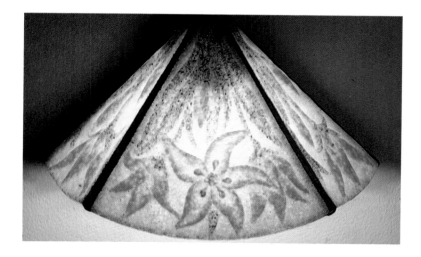

74   Wall-bracket
The three-part wall-bracket, made of *pâte-de-verre*, depicts stylized red tulips, either partially closed or open to reveal the stamens.
~ 1900
H: 15.5 cm   W: 40 cm

Jean-Auguste Dampt

Sculptor, born in Venarcy in 1853. Year of death unknown. He was a pupil of Jouffroy and P. Dubois at the Académie des Beaux-Arts in Paris. In Italy he learned the *cire-perdue* method of casting bronze, but initially continued to work in marble. He loved fine materials: ivory, gold, steel, and silver, which he combined, together with white, rose-coloured, grey and black marbles from Siena, and he endeavoured to remain true to these materials when working them up into objects. In collaboration with Serrurier, he exhibited chandeliers and wall-brackets in the Palais de l'Electricité at the World Exhibition in 1900. The forms of his pieces were drawn from nature: bunches of flower- or tree-stems, for example, made from copper or bronze. His light-bulb settings consist of crowns of flowers or other floral motifs.

75   Wall-bracket
Bronze, with two narcissus buds and an illuminated flower. Opaline and white acid-etched glass.
~ 1900
H: 90 cm   Ø: 27 cm

76 *Ceiling-light*
Gilt bronze with five columbine
blooms and three buds.
~ 1900
H: 96 cm   ∅: 75 cm

Daum Frères

The world-famous firm, which still exists today under the name Cristalleries de Nancy, was founded in 1875 as the Verrerie de Nancy. The firm was taken over in 1887 by the two brothers Auguste (1853-1909) and Antonin Daum (1864-1930), the latter assuming artistic direction. The firm had no style of its own up until 1889, but was inspired by Gallé's success at the Paris World Exhibition in that year, and changed over to the production of art glass. In 1891 followed the founding of the Ateliers d'Art à la Verrerie de Nancy which had apprentice workshops for glass technicians, polishers, etchers, painters and gilders. Around 1893 Daum Frères produced their first etched vases in overlay technique with floral and figurative designs or landscapes. At the same time they first began to use glass powder melted in or on the glass (Jade glass). Around 1900 important artists such as Henri Bergé, Damman and Emile Wirtz were working as painters and designers for the firm. Adolphe Claude and Eugène Gall worked as glassmakers, Sévère, Winckler, Jules Marchand and Racadot as polishers and engravers and, after 1898,

Jacques Gruber as designer and painter of windows.

Daum Frères took part in many world exhibitions between 1889 and 1925, and won international acclaim in 1900 at the Paris World Exhibition. Antonin Daum became a Knight of the Legion of Honour and his firm was awarded the Grand Prix.

Between 1905 and 1930 the Daum Brothers worked together with other craftsmen such as Edgar Brandt, André Groult, Louis Majorelle and the Nics Brothers, who made the iron mounts for Daum glass. Between 1908 and 1914 Almaric Walter produced many objects, including lampshades, out of *pâte-de-verre*, after designs by Henri Bergé. The production of art glass followed a new direction after 1911 with the manufacture of heavy thick-walled vessels of austere shape, and bearing etched decorative motifs after about 1920.

The influence of Emile Gallé can be detected in certain productions by Daum Frères, but their lamps are unmistakably their own: distinctive in both shape and colour.

77 *Hanging lamp*
The three *pâte-de-verre* globes are decorated with green glass drops.
~ 1898
Sign. Daum/Nancy
H: 50 cm   Ø: 15 cm

78 *Ceiling-light*
Cased glass (two layers) decorated with red and brown flowers and leaves. Fixture of wrought iron (Majorelle ?).
~ 1900
H: 55 cm   Ø: 36 cm

79 *Hanging lamp with two wall-brackets*
Yellow, brown and red *pâte-de-verre* with a marbled effect. The canopy, richly decorated in gilded bronze with a design of cherry fruit and leaves, carries four small shades. The wall-lights are similarly decorated with gilded bronze and have *pâte-de-verre* shades.
~ 1899
All glass parts are signed Daum/Nancy. The bronze is signed Demarco
Hanging lamp:
H: 100 cm   Ø: 80 cm
Wall-bracket:
H: 52 cm   Ø: 44 cm

80 *Table-lamp*
Glass enclosing coloured powders. Base and shade with applied glass teardrops. Both illuminated.
~ 1902
Sign. Daum/Nancy
H: 38 cm   Ø: 20 cm

82 *Table-lamp*
Multi-layered glass etched with a design of wild vinefruits and leaves. Colours: brown, green and yellow.
~ 1900
Sign. Daum/Nancy
H: 43 cm   Ø: 32 cm

81 *Ceiling-light*
Hanging on four chains; cased glass with inclusions of coloured powder; decorated with a wild vine motif.
~ 1900
Sign. Daum/Nancy, France
Ø: 48 cm

83   *Table-lamp*
Glass coloured with red and
orange powder and blown into an
iron frame in such a way as to
represent a ring of mandarin
oranges. Base of hammered
wrought iron by Edgar Brandt.
~ 1920
Sign. Daum/Nancy (Shade)
Sign. E. Brandt (Base)
H: 52.5 cm   ∅: 32 cm
Lit. Victor Arwas, *Glass Art
Nouveau to Art Deco*, p. 56

84   *Table-lamp*
Cased glass with powder
inclusions, in blue, brown, green
and lilac, acid-etched and
engraved with a design of an
autumn landscape.
~ 1899
Sign. Daum/Nancy
H: 37 cm   ∅: 20 cm

85   *Table-lamp*
Cased glass with powder
inclusions, acid-etched and
engraved with a design of a
spring landscape.
~ 1899
Sign. Daum/Nancy
H: 37 cm   ∅: 20 cm

86   *Table-lamp*
Cased glass with powder
inclusions, acid-etched and
engraved with a design of a
summer landscape. Colours:
brown and green.
~ 1899
Sign. Daum/Nancy
H: 37 cm   ∅: 20 cm

87   *Table-lamp*
Cased glass (three layers) etched
and engraved with a design of
foliage and dark berries. Both
base and shade are illuminated.
~ 1900
Sign. Daum/Nancy
H: 56 cm   ∅: 28 cm

88   *Table-lamp*
Cased glass (three layers) in
green, white, pink and yellow,
etched and engraved with
branches of cherry blossom. Both
the base and the mushroom-
shaped shade are illuminated.
~ 1898
Sign. Daum/Nancy
H: 60.5 cm   ∅: 29.5 cm

89 *Table-lamp*
Cased glass with *martelé*-like
etching in a chestnut-leaf design.
Base and shade are illuminated.
Colours: blue, yellow, white.
~1910
Sign. Daum/Nancy
H: 38 cm   Ø: 19 cm

90 *Table-lamp*
Cased glass (three layers), etched
and engraved with blue tendrils
and leaves, with a *martelé* finish.
~ 1900
Sign. Daum/Nancy
H: 46 cm   Ø: 12 cm

91 *Table-lamp*
Light-blue and brown cased glass
(two layers), engraved with a
design of sea creatures (on the
inside of the shade) and seaweed
(on the outside). Both the base
and the mushroom-shaped shade
are illuminated.
1900
Engraved signature Daum/
Nancy
H: 45 cm   Ø: 23 cm

92 *Table-lamp*
Cased glass (three layers) with a
partial *martelé* finish and a design
of a mistletoe twig. Colours: red,
yellow, blue.
~ 1900
Sign. Daum/Nancy
H: 45 cm   Ø: 15 cm

93 *Small table-lamp*
Violet, brown and yellow cased
glass (three layers) with a
decoration of flowering lilies.
Both shade and base are
illuminated. The frame is of
wrought iron.
~ 1900
Sign. Daum/Nancy
H: 32 cm   Ø: 14 cm

94 *Table-lamp*
The bronze base is decorated
with a design of wild convulvulus.
The *pâte-de-verre* shades have
been coloured with powder and
carry a geometrical pattern.
Sign. Daum/Nancy
H: 58 cm   Ø: 4 cm

95 *Table-lamp*
Deeply etched yellowish glass.
Both shade and base are
illuminated.
~ 1928
Sign. Daum, France
H: 65 cm   Ø: 27 cm

96 *Small table-lamp*
Base of hammered wrought iron.
Spherical shade supporting a
small cupola. The glass has been
coloured with melted metal
threads.
~ 1910
Sign. Daum/Nancy
H: 15 cm   Ø: 11 cm

97   *Table-lamp*
Cased glass with powder
colouration, etched and engraved
with a winter landscape: on the
shade, trees and a pool with
mountains in the background; on
the base, a continuation of the
tree motifs. Colours: blue, brown
and green. Both shade and base
are illuminated.
~ 1899
Sign. Daum/Nancy
H: 57 cm   Ø: 20 cm

98   *Table-lamp*
Multi-layered glass in green,
brown, yellow and red, etched
and engraved with a design of
fishing boats on the shade and an
abstract motif on the base. Both
the base and the triangular-
shaped shade are illuminated.
~ 1896
Sign. Daum/Nancy
H: 43 cm
Ill. Blount, *French Cameo Glass*,
p. 130, Ill. No. 232c

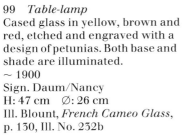

99   *Table-lamp*
Cased glass in yellow, brown and
red, etched and engraved with a
design of petunias. Both base and
shade are illuminated.
~ 1900
Sign. Daum/Nancy
H: 47 cm   ∅: 26 cm
Ill. Blount, *French Cameo Glass*,
p. 130, Ill. No. 232b

100   *Table-lamp*
Cased glass coloured with
powder and oxides. Colours: red,
yellow, white. Both the base and
the mushroom-shaped shade are
illuminated.
~1910
Sign. Daum/Nancy
H: 60 cm   ∅: 24.3 cm

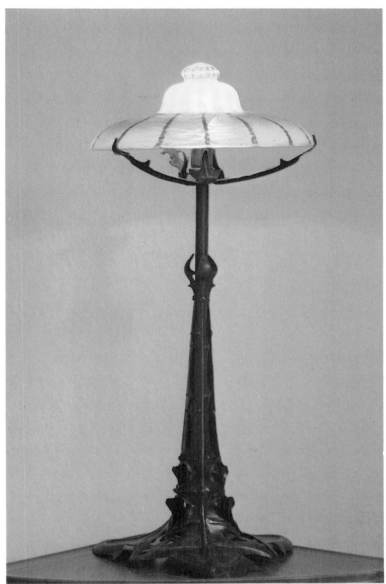

101 *Small table-lamp*
On a slender base, a spherical
shade of green, blue and orange
cased glass, etched and engraved
with a design of orange-leaves
and having a *martelé* finish.
~ 1898
Sign. Daum/Nancy
H: 46 cm

102 *Table-lamp*
A bronze base with a thistle
design supports the double-
cupola shade made of cased glass
with powder inclusions.
Colours: green, yellow, pink.
~ 1896
Sign. Daum/Nancy
H: 60 cm   Ø: 18 cm

103 *Table-lamp*
Glass with powder inclusions.
Frame of wrought iron
1905
Sign. Daum/Nancy
H: 40 cm ∅: 16 cm

104 *Table-lamp*
Cased glass with an abstract
decoration. Colours: green,
yellow. Both base and shade are
illuminated.
~ 1910
Sign. Daum/Nancy
H: 59 cm ∅: 30 cm

105 *Table-lamp*
Iron base with a thistle design
that is repeated in etching on the
cased-glass shade. Colours:
yellow and brown.
1898
Sign. Daum/Nancy
Base: Majorelle (?)
H: 37 cm ∅: 17 cm

106 *Table-lamp*
The base is cone-shaped polished
steel, opening out towards the
top. The shade is etched glass.
~ 1930
Sign. Daum/Nancy, France
H: 64 cm ∅: 41 cm

107 *Table-lamp*
The bronze base represents a
flower. The brown, orange and
violet cased-glass shade has a
design of flying bats.
~ 1899
Sign. Majorelle (Base)
Daum/Nancy (Shade)
H: 76 cm ∅: 34 cm

108 *Table-lamp*
Red, green and yellow cased glass
(three layers) with a design of
flowering columbines and a
partial *martelé* finish.
~ 1900
H: 42 cm ∅: 14 cm

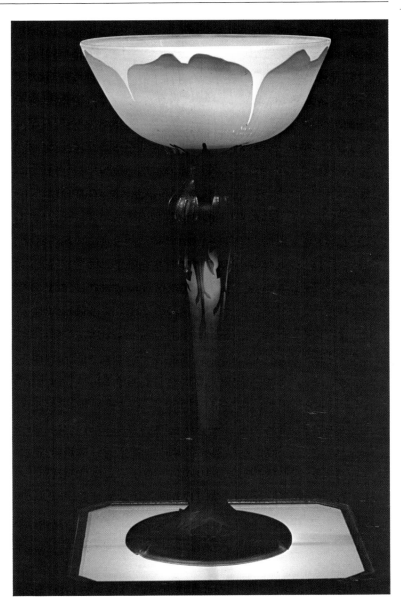

109 *Table-lamp*
Bronze base with plant-like
decoration, carrying an
illuminated *pâte-de-verre* bloom.
~ 1898
Base: Louis Majorelle. Glass:
Daum Frères
H: 62 cm Ø: 18 cm

110 *Table-lamp*
Cased glass in pink, dark green
and blue, etched with a plant-like
design. Both base and shade are
illuminated.
~ 1900
Sign. Daum/Nancy
H: 34 cm Ø: 34 cm

112 *Table-lamp*
Pink, red, green and black multi-
layered glass, etched and wheel-
carved. The shade is in the shape
of an open flower; the base
carries an abstract design. Both
base and shade are illuminated.
1904
Sign. Daum/Nancy
H: 80 cm Ø: 36.5 cm
Antonin Daum produced only one
finished example of this lamp, a
wedding present for his daughter.
A trial piece is in a private
collection in Paris.

111 *Table lamp*
Cased glass with powder
inclusions, etched in part with a
design of a climbing plant. Both
shade and base are illuminated.
~ 1900
Sign. Daum/Nancy
H: 41 cm Ø: 19 cm

113 Table-lamp
Cut and etched glass with an
abstract design. Both shade and
base are illuminated.
1925
Sign. Daum/Nancy, France
H: 52 cm   Ø: 40 cm

114 Table-lamp
Etched glass. Both base and
shade are illuminated.
~ 1930
Sign. Daum
H: 51.5 cm   Ø: 13 cm

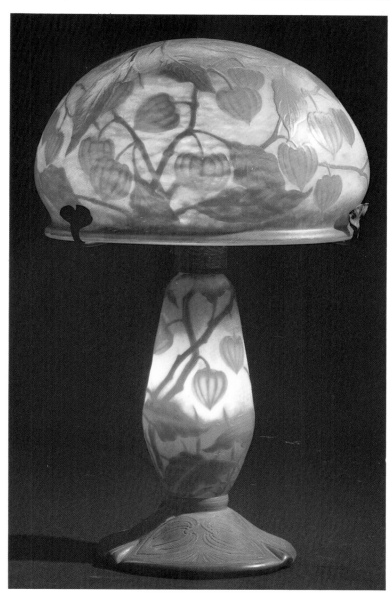

115   *Table-lamp*
Single-coloured *pâte-de-verre*
with etched abstract design.
~1924
Sign. Daum/Nancy, France
H: 63 cm   Ø: 32 cm

116   *Table-lamp*
Red, yellow and green cased glass
(three layers), etched and
engraved with Chinese-lantern
flowers. Both base and shade are
illuminated.
~ 1900
Sign. Daum/Nancy
H: 52 cm   Ø: 33 cm

Georges de Feure

Of Dutch-Belgian descent, de Feure lived and died in Paris (1868-1928). He was a pupil of Jules Chéret in Paris in 1890. Influenced by Eugène Grasset and by Japanese art, he began his artistic career designing theatre sets and working as a newspaper illustrator. After 1894 he regularly took part in exhibitions mounted by the Société Nationale des Beaux-Arts and in 1896 he exhibited at the Munich Secession Exhibition in Germany.

Many outstanding pieces by de Feure were to be seen at Bing's Maison de l'Art Nouveau from its inception.

His enthusiasm for the decorative arts led de Feure to experiment with a whole range of materials, which demanded of him new and specialized skills. His works in wood, ivory, porcelain, glass, bronze, silver, paper, wool and silk are considered today as masterpieces of the French Art Nouveau style, on which he left a most definite mark, and his paintings figure prominently in many great collections. De Feure's work can perhaps best be compared, for range and quality, with that of the Belgian van de Velde.

117 *Pair of candlesticks*
Double-armed, gilt bronze with stylized floral design. The candlesticks are adapted for use with either electricity or candles.
~ 1905
Sign. DE FEURE
H: 25 cm   W: 34 cm
⌀: 15 cm (Base)

118 *Candlestick*
Silvered bronze. Base in an abstract floral design.
~ 1900
H: 35 cm

119 *Candlestick*
Gilt bronze. Water-lily design.
Sign. DE FEURE
H: 15 cm   W: 23 cm
Ill. *Art et Décoration* (1901), p. 83

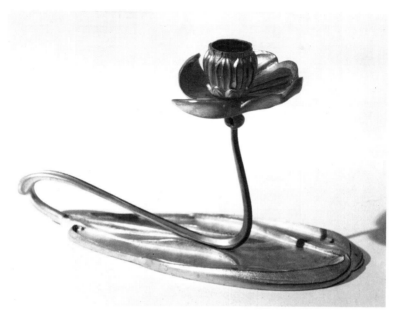

120 *Candelabrum*
Three branches, silvered brass.
~ 1900
H: 38 cm   W: 26 cm
Ill. *Art et Décoration* (1901), p. 82

122 *Candlestick*
Bronze. Representing a stylized
flower bud.
Sign. DE FEURE
H: 28 cm

121 *Candlestick*
Silvered bronze. Base in a stylized
flower design.
1900
H: 28.5 cm
Ill. *Art et Décoration*, IX (1901),
p. 87

123 *Candlestick*
Gilt bronze, in the shape of a
stylized flower.
H: 25.5 cm

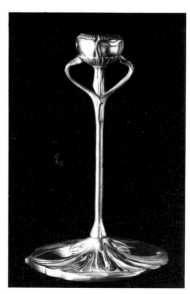

André Delatte

Dates unknown. In 1921 he founded a glassworks in Nancy, which subsequently became known for its production of cased glass, etched, in particular, with flowers and landscapes.

124   *Decorative lamp*
Coloured and etched glass with applied enamel. Abstract design. The fixture lifts the egg-shaped peak about 0.5 cm above the rest of the lamp. Base of hammered wrought iron.
Sign. Delatte, Nancy
H: 15 cm   ∅: 9 cm

Felix Del Marle

(1889-1952). In 1912 he got to know Apollinaire and Severini, who introduced him to the Italian Futurists. He identified wholeheartedly with the principles and techniques of Futurism and in 1913 published a Futurist manifesto in the Parisian newspaper *Le Jour*. After his return from the First World War, Del Marle devoted his abilities to caricature and it was not until he met Kupka in 1920 that he began painting seriously. Two years later he took an enthusiastic interest in Mondrian's work and joined the De Stijl group. He produced a magazine *Vouloir*, which later became the *Revue Mensuelle d'Esthétique Néo-Plastique*. Influenced by Mondrian's Neo-Plasticism, Del Marle sought to carry it over into everyday life: colour, he claimed, should go below the surface of objects to express their architectural reality. In the complete interiors and furniture he designed, he accorded great importance to colour: "It is essential", he said, "that colour contributes in linking the collective life of a city with the individual lives of its citizens, not on the level of economic necessity, but on the higher plane of order, balance and therefore beauty."

125 *Floor-lamp*
Part of the *Mobilier Néo-Plastique*.
Painted wood, wrought iron and
painted, matt glass.
1926
H: ~ 160 cm

126 *Floor-lamp*
Three-cornered base in oak and
iron, painted black and white;
shade of white etched glass in the
shape of a half-open umbrella.
1926
H: 184 cm

Maurice Dufrène

Born in Paris in 1876, died in Nogent-sur-Marne in 1955. After extensive studies at the Ecole des Arts Décoratifs in Paris, he joined Meier-Gräfe's Maison Moderne in 1899. Of this period he later (1921) wrote: "My experience there brought me an exhaustive knowledge of my clients' needs in terms of all-round furnishing. This serious contact with industry was my real and definitive education as an interior designer."

In 1902 Dufrène played an active part in the foundation of the Société des Artistes Décorateurs. After 1910 he exhibited furniture, wallpapers, carpets, jewellery, ceramics and art glass in a number of salons. As a professor at the Ecole Boulle (1912-25) he was an enthusiastic advocate of a variety of industrial techniques, and he also published numerous articles, particularly in *Art et Décoration*, the monthly modern-art magazine dealing with the applied arts and especially with interiors and furnishings.

1920 saw the founding of La Maîtrise, a furnishing studio attached to the large department store Les Galeries Lafayettes, whose studios at that time played an operative role in introducing new furnishing ideas to an otherwise inexperienced public. Maurice Dufrène, who directed La Maîtrise until 1940, employed the most diverse materials – wood, stoneware (in collaboration with Dalpayrat), metal and leather – in his furnishing designs. He was elected vice-president of the Salon d'Automne and a Knight of the Legion of Honour. The Compagnie des Arts Français exhibited a number of his chandeliers and wall-brackets. Of his lamps, the periodical *Art et Décoration* wrote in an article about the Salon d'Automne in 1913: "Apart from his interiors, Dufrène also exhibited electric lamps made of decorated gilded bronze, like flowers, rising up in lovely rhythmical motion, on straight or sinuous stems." See also Documentation.

127　*Table-lamp*
Base of polished bronze in an abstract design. The sides of the shade are stretched fabric; the top is set with coloured glass pieces in lead.
1913
Sign. Maurice Dufrène
H: 82 cm　∅: 54 cm

Paul Follot

Born in Paris in 1877, died in Sainte-Maxime in 1941. He worked for a few years at Meier-Gräfe's Maison Moderne and by 1904 was already well known as a sculptor and decorator. His first designs show a strong Pre-Raphaelite influence. He preferred to work with costly materials: inlays, lacquer and bronze. His most important works include interiors, carpets, wallpapers and china. Follot was known as the defender of aristocratic tradition in the sense of individual luxury, and was opposed to art produced in series.

128 *Candlestick*
Three-branched, silvered bronze. Stylized flower design on base and sockets.
~ 1904
Sign. Follot, Paris
H: 31 cm   W: 21 cm

Emile Gallé

Born and died in Nancy (1846-1904). Gallé's work was central to the formation of the Jugendstil or Art Nouveau. The medium through which he expressed his combination of aesthetic, literary, artistic, philosophical and even natural-scientific principles was glass. Although he mastered a variety of other materials, such as ceramics and furniture inlays, glass remained his true means of expression; while on his own doorstep in Nancy, Daum Frères were also experimenting with glass, Gallé was producing pieces with his own unmistakable stamp.

His lamps are individual creations in glass that is designed exclusively for the purpose of illumination. Even those models which were produced in larger series avoid the repetitive and the uniform. Only a few Gallé candlesticks are known today; they are made either of faïence or silver.

There was a long-standing tradition of glass and ceramic production in Gallé's family. Since 1845 Emile's father Charles Gallé-Reinemer had owned a series of glass refineries and also faïence works in Raon-L'Etapes and Saint-Clément. Emile Gallé studied rhetoric, philosophy and botany from 1862 until 1865, and then mineralogy between 1865 and 1866 in Weimar. This was followed (until the end of 1867) by a period of theoretical and practical training in the glassworks belonging to the firm of Burgun Schverer & Co., Meisenthal, the suppliers of raw glass to his father. Gallé had his own glass laboratory in Meisenthal as early as 1867. After 1870 he worked in his father's faïence factory in Saint-Clément and got to know there Victor Prouvé who later became one of his closest friends and colleagues. He spent the year 1871 travelling to London and Paris where he visited museums and botanical gardens. After the end of the Franco-Prussian War, in 1871, Meisenthal, together with Elsass-Lothringen, belonged to Germany. This induced Gallé to build his own small factory in Nancy, and to expand the existing refineries there. The faïence works were also moved from Saint-Clément to Nancy in 1874. Emile Gallé took over their

direction. In 1878 he took part, for the first time, in the Paris World Exhibition, with enamelled and cut-glass objects, made after Oriental and Asian models, and won four gold medals. He founded a workshop for the manufacture of inlayed furniture in Nancy in 1883.

In 1884 at the "Union Centrale" Exhibition, he exhibited parti-coloured glass with areas of infused metal foil, as well as multiple overlay and inlayed-glass imitations of semi-precious stones, and floral designs following studies in nature. He liked to accentuate the symbolical potential of his glass objects with quotations from poetry and literature (*verrerie parlante*). From 1885 until 1896 a private contract was in force between Burgun Schverer & Co. and Gallé. The firm pledged itself to produce Gallé's commissions exactly to his instructions. The designs were carried out in the workshops of the painter Désiré Christian; the technical processes worked out in Gallé's scientific laboratories were kept a close secret.

In 1893 he took part in the Chicago World Exhibition. After 1897 he exhibited his first objects with partly applied and partly inlayed glass (*marqueterie de verre*). The Paris World Exhibitions of 1889 and 1900 reflected high points in his artistic achievement. Gallé won many gold medals, various Grand Prix and was named a Knight of the Legion of Honour. He employed at this time about three hundred workers. In 1901 Gallé founded the soon famous Ecole de Nancy, whose members included: Emile Gallé, Louis Majorelle, Antonin and Jean-Auguste Daum, Eugène Vallin, Georges Hoentschel and Victor Prouvé. In 1902 Gallé took part in the World Exhibition in Turin.

Emile Gallé died on 23 September 1904. His son-in-law, the art historian Paul Perdrizet, took over the directorship of the firm which he kept going through the mass production of old models. There was no further artistic development. Victor Prouvé took over as leader of the Ecole de Nancy. The claim that a star was added to Gallé's signature after his death is not proven: there are many examples of pieces produced between

1904 and 1925 which bear the signature "Gallé" without any further addition. After 1920 the firm styled itself "Etablissement Gallé". The factory was closed down in 1931, and shortly afterwards all the workshops were destroyed.

129 *Ceiling-lamp*
Globe-shaped. Etched and engraved cased glass with a nasturtium motif. Colours: brown, yellow, red.
~ 1899
Sign. Gallé
⌀: 36 cm

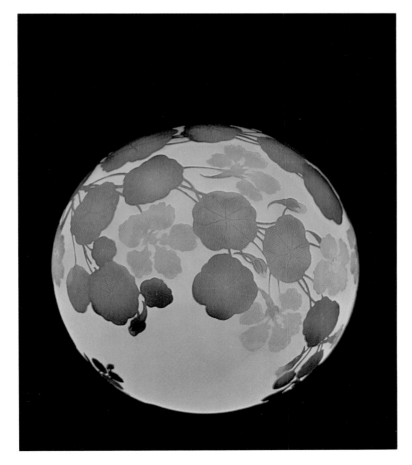

130 *Table-lamp*
Etched and engraved cased glass. On the base: a landscape with trees; on the shade: flying bats. Base and shade both illuminated.
~ 1900
Sign. Gallé
H: 57.5 cm   ⌀: 24 cm

133 *Table-lamp*
Glass with several overlays.
Colours: brown, yellow, white;
etched and engraved with a
design of vine leaves and yellow
marguerites. Base and shade
both illuminated.
~ 1900
Sign. Gallé
H: 68 cm   Ø: 39 cm

131 *Small table-lamp*
Wheel-carved and etched cased
glass in yellow and red, with a
design of red and light-red wild
roses, birds and butterflies. Both
the three-cornered shade and the
bulbous base are illuminated.
~ 1895
Sign. Gallé
H: 26 cm

132 *Table-lamp*
Cased glass partly striped with
powder inclusions, etched and
engraved with a design of box
leaves and various flowers.
Colours: yellow, brown, blue and
pink. Shade and base both
illuminated.
Sign. Gallé
H: 60 cm   Ø: 35 cm

134 *Table-lamp*
Cased glass. Maple leaves and
fruit etched and engraved on base
and shade. Shade and base both
illuminated.
~ 1900
Sign. Gallé
H: 59 cm   Ø: 37 cm

137 *Table-lamp*
Yellow and carnelian cased glass, etched with a design of magnolias. Both base and shade are illuminated.
~ 1900
Sign. E. Gallé
H: 61 cm   Ø: 31 cm

135 *Table-lamp*
Cased glass (three layers). Yellow, brown, red. Etched and engraved with a design of flowering rhododendron. Shade and base both illuminated.
~ 1900
Sign. Gallé
H: 48 cm   Ø: 34 cm

136 *Table-lamp*
Mushroom-shaped; multi-layered glass. The round base and the shade are decorated with a leaf pattern and blue flowers. Both shade and base are illuminated.
Sign. Gallé
H: 31 cm   Ø: 30 cm

138 *Table-lamp*
Glass blown in a mould, overlaid, etched and engraved with a design of cherry branches. Colours: red, brown, yellow. Shade and base both illuminated.
Sign. Gallé
H: 47 cm   Ø: 31 cm

141 *Table-lamp*
Cased glass. The design on foot and shade is of wild plum twigs with fruit. Colours: blue, yellow.
~ 1902
Sign. Gallé
H: 68 cm   Ø: 38 cm

142 *Small table-lamp*
Etched and engraved case glass, with Japanese-style motifs. The base depicts a butterfly, the shade flowering twigs in a dish.
Colours: blue, brown, yellow, green. Shade and base both illuminated.
~ 1896
Sign. Gallé
H: 26 cm   Ø: 30 cm

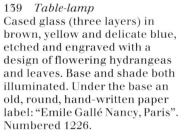

139 *Table-lamp*
Cased glass (three layers) in brown, yellow and delicate blue, etched and engraved with a design of flowering hydrangeas and leaves. Base and shade both illuminated. Under the base an old, round, hand-written paper label: "Emile Gallé Nancy, Paris". Numbered 1226.
~ 1901
Sign. Gallé
H: 44 cm

140 *Table-lamp*
Cased glass with inclusions of yellow, red and gold. The urn-shaped body of the lamp stands on a silver base. The decorative handle is also silver.
~ 1900
Sign. Gallé (Glass)
Sign. Arsler & Co., Paris (Silver)
H: 23 cm   Ø: 11 cm

143 *Table-lamp*
Cased glass. Design on base: landscape with trees; on shade: flying swallows. Etched and engraved. Colours: brown, orange, white. Shade and base are both illuminated.
~ 1898
Sign. Gallé
H: 68 cm   Ø: 28 cm

146 *Small table-lamp*
Pink, green and carnelian-red *marqueterie de verre*. The flower-shaped shade and polished shaft have been cast in a mould, then overlaid with carnelian; the flower petals are veined. The base is mounted in gilded bronze with a mistletoe design.
~ 1897
Vertical, moulded signature on the shaft: E. Gallé
H: 36 cm
Ill. Bloch-Dermant, *L'Art du verre en France 1860-1914*, p. 91

144 *Ceiling-lamp*
Etched cased glass in two colours: white and reddish brown.
~ 1900
Sign. Gallé
H: 40 cm (with chains)
Ø: 15 cm (Shade)

145 *Table-lamp*
Cased glass coloured with metal oxides. Motif: sea creatures and seaweed. Colours: brown, yellow, red, violet, white. Shade and base both illuminated.
~ 1898
Sign. Gallé
H: 18 cm   Ø: 20 cm

147 *Table-lamp*
Wrought-iron stand that
continues up around the glass
shaft. The fixture is also wrought
iron. The undulating shade
represents a hemlock flower.
Beige, yellow and green cased
glass, etched and engraved.
~ 1900
Sign. Gallé
H: 77 cm   Ø: 40 cm

148 *Table-lamp*
The gilt-bronze base is composed
of four leaves supporting a
flower-shaped frame. The shade
is cased glass with a design of
leaf veins.
Sign. Colonna (Base)
Gallé (Shade)
H: 47 cm   Ø: 13 cm

149 *Table-lamp*
Coloured glass, etched with gold
and enamel applications. The
abstract design is based on
Islamic motifs.
~ 1898
Sign. Gallé
H: 35 cm   Ø: 20 cm

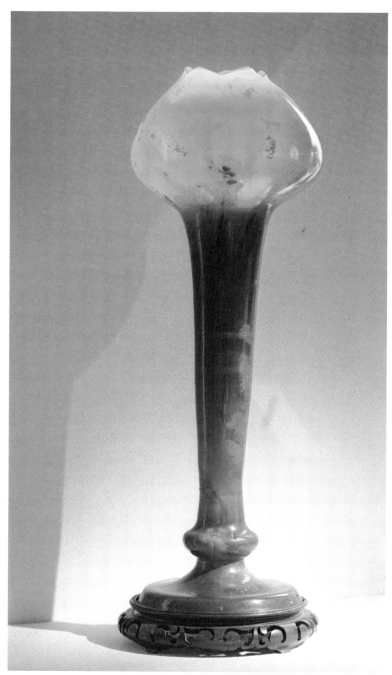

150 *Decorative lamp*
Cased glass coloured with oxides
on a carved wooden base. The
lamp is in one piece and depicts a
flower. The orange part of the
shade is engraved with petals.
~ 1900
Sign. Emile Gallé
Catalogue Kunstmuseum
Düsseldorf

151 *Ceiling-lamp*
Yellow glass overlaid in green,
with a design of leaf veins.
Sign. Gallé
H: 32 cm   Ø: 32 cm

152 *Decorative lamp*
Les Coprins; in the shape of three
mushrooms on a gilded iron base,
which represents a stylized forest
floor. The three stalks are made
of a striped and twisted grey
glass. The smallest mushroom is
closed up, the middle-sized and
largest caps are open at the
bottom and have a wavy edge.
Colours: grey, yellow, brown.
Only four variants of this lamp are
known. They were originally
commissioned for a dining room
whose decor was based on
woodland flora.
One of these variants was
auctioned in Geneva in 1985 for
over 400.000 dollars.
Sign. Gallé
H: 83 cm

153 *Floor-lamp*
The wooden base and shaft have
bronze mounts. The shade is
etched and engraved cased glass
with leaves, flowers and a group
of birds.
~ 1902
Shade sign. Gallé, who also made
the base
H: 205 cm   ∅: 63 cm

154 *Pair of candlesticks*
A pair of heraldic lions rampant each hold a tower with five turrets for the candles. On the towers are shields with the Den Haag coat-of-arms. The lions' heads are slightly turned to one side and they have gaping jaws; their very long tails are wound several times around the body. The high oval base is also glazed on the underside, has rounded edges and a lively intertwining scroll design at the front. Dark-red clay with a whitish-blue glaze, light and dark-blue underglaze, decorated with iron-red, black and gold after Far Eastern models. The five-branched candelabrum is made of brass.
1879
Sign. Gallé Editeur Nancy
H: 41 cm (including candelabrum: 69 cm)
W: 25 cm

156 *Table-lamp*
Wrought-iron base with leaf design. The etched cased-glass shades are decorated with light-blue and greenish flowers.
~ 1900
Sign. Bartheleme (Base)
Sign. Gallé (Shade)
H: 55 cm Ø: 13 cm

155 *Candlestick*
Richly decorated with a plant-like design. Marked: Gallia-Métal 4367. Design: Gallé. Sign.: rhombus with a he-goat's head turned to the left.
~ 1900
H: 25 cm
Ill. *Le Modern Style*, pp. 152-53

Jean Goulden

Born in Charpenty (Meuse) in 1878, died in
Reims in 1947. He came from a rich Alsatian
family of agriculturalists. After being awarded
distinctions at the Ecole Alsacienne, he went on
to study medicine in Paris, where, as both painter
and musician (and also sponsor) he was a
member of the Montmartre movement and got
to know a number of great artists. He produced a
thesis on the physiology of the heart and
practised medicine as a visiting doctor at Paris
hospitals. During the First World War he was a
company doctor on the Macedonian front. At the
end of the war, he stayed as a guest for some
months at a monastery on Mount Athos, where
he discovered the beauty of Byzantine enamel
paintings. On his return home to France he once
again met Jean Dunand, who introduced him to
the technique of *cloisonné* enamel. In the
meanwhile he continued to sponsor the group of
artists who exhibited with him regularly in the
Galerie Georges Petit: Dunand, Jouve and
Schmied, whose daughter he married in 1925.
He kept his studio and his furnace in Paris until
1927.
After 1928 he lived in Reims where he continued
his work.

157　*Table-lamp*
Silvered bronze and enamel.
1929
Sign. Jean Goulden, with the
number XCIX
H: 33.5 cm

Eileen Gray

Born in Ireland in 1878 and year of death was
1977. After studying for three years in London's
Soho, where she learned the technique of
lacquering, she finally settled in Paris in 1902.
She perfected her knowledge of lacquering
under the Japanese lacquerer Sougawara (who
also advised Jean Dunand). Her classical
training did not prevent her, however, from
inventing a striking new style: "My idea was to
create things which were in accordance with our
time. We lived in an unbelievably old-fashioned
climate," she later said. Only single pieces of
furniture were ever produced from her designs,
in spite of her wish for serial production.
Eileen Gray opened her own shop – the Galerie
Jean Désert – in 1922, where everything on
display was designed by herself, and executed in
three workshops.
She designed her first tubular-steel furniture in
1925-26 at the same time as Marcel Breuer and
Mies van der Rohe and, also in 1926, a folding
chair made of lacquered wood for use on a
transatlantic liner.In 1927 she devoted her
energies to architecture, working in
collaboration with Jean Badovici. Together they
realized a number of large projects, daringly
conceived and aimed at improving the standard
of living. "A house is a living organism; its
interior design cannot be the fortuitous result of
the façade, but must arise out of the overall,
harmonious and logical life of the house. The
plan should by no means be subordinate to the
exterior, on the contrary, it should determine it,"
she explained. She attempted in this way to
create a life style, in which everything was
dictated by comfort.

158 *Floor-lamp*
Laquered wood. Parchment
shade.
~ 1922
H: 189 cm

Hector Guimard

Born in 1867, died in New York in 1942. Became known around 1890 as an architect and designer. He designed chimney-pieces, lamps, furniture, wallpapers, door- and window handles. In 1899 he designed the world-famous entrances to the Paris Metro. In the latter designs, Guimard made extensive use of cast iron, but the green colour, with which the iron was painted, was found by Parisians to be obstrusively "Germanic". His buildings are pioneers of the period, culminating in the Castel Béranger and the Humbert de Romans concert hall (1897-1901), now only to be seen in photographs. After the First World War Guimard's work was forgotten. He left France in 1938.

159 *Hanging lamp*
Gilded bronze. Cords with glass balls, glass and bronze rods. Four shields at the side made of pale-blue *pâte-de-verre*.
~ 1895
Sign. Guimard
H: 46 cm Ø: 21 cm

160 *Hanging lamp*
Bronze, glass rods, crystal cords and four shield-shaped side-pieces made of dull-etched glass. The lamp was shown at the World Exhibition in Ostend.
H: 100 cm Ø: 55 cm

161 *Wall-light with a mirror*
Gilded bronze. Hollow-glass and bronze rods are suspended from the crown.
~ 1895
H: 22 cm (with mirror: 83 cm)
Ø: 9.5 cm

René Lalique

Born in Ay, Marne, in 1860, died in Paris in 1945. Lalique became famous worldwide for a whole variety of artistic creations. He was both a unique gold- and silversmith, a craftsman in enamel, glass and precious stones, and a brilliant designer in other areas of the applied arts too. His career matches this versatility. In 1876/77 he was apprenticed to a goldsmith and studied at the Ecole des Arts Décoratifs in Paris. From 1878 to 1880 he continued his studies at Sydenham College in England. In 1886 he furnished his own goldsmith workshop in Paris. Lalique was represented for the first time at the World Exhibition in Paris in 1899 by a small collection of jewellery. After 1890 he began to search for a convincing way of combining metal, *pâte-de-verre* and precious stones. In 1897 Lalique became a member of the Société des Artistes Français and Knight of the Legion of Honour. His first works in opaline with silver mounts appeared in 1898. He worked in close collaboration with Samuel Bing (1838-1905) at the latter's Maison de l'Art Nouveau, became friendly with Alphonse Mucha (1860-1939) and exercized a definite influence on his pupil Eugène Feuillâtre (1870-1916). The Paris World Exhibition in 1900 brought him great acclaim. As a designer and creator of jewellery, for Sarah Bernhardt among others, Lalique surpassed all the other exhibitors.

The most beautiful collection of his jewellery is to be found today in the Gulbenkian Museum in Lisbon.

1900 also saw his increased interest in glass and the art of gem-cutting. After 1902 Lalique worked with four glassmakers on a stove of his own design in Clairefontaine. Production here principally involved unique pieces in the *cire-perdue* method, such as flat reliefs of coloured glass for chandeliers, lamps, door panels and jewellery boxes. In 1907 Lalique designed perfume bottles for Côty, Worth, Morabito, Forvil and Roger & Gallet, amongst others. He transferred the execution of his designs to the Legras & Cie glassworks, and between 1908 and 1909 he founded his own glassworks, the Verrerie de Combs-la-Ville in Combs. Vases, lamps, plaques and pieces of jewellery with designs in relief, or engraved and occasionally enamelled motifs were produced there. In 1912 Lalique set up his own exhibition in Paris. A year later he gave up his activities as a jeweller for good. Between 1918 and 1922, a second, larger glassworks was established in Wingen-sur-Moder, the Verreries d'Alsace René Lalique & Cie. Here monochrome, moulded glass was made to his own designs. From now on, each piece was marked "R. Lalique France" and often also with the model number.

The great applied arts exhibition in Paris, the "Exposition des Arts Décoratifs et Industriels Modernes" of 1925, celebrated Lalique as the greatest living glass artist. He had a Pavilion of his own at the exhibition, where a fountain and triumphal arch caused a particular sensation, as did a dining room with table decorations and various lamps made for the Sèvres manufacturers. From that time to the present day, the Lalique firm has produced a variety of art glass, figurines, sculpture and glass parts for use in architecture. The glassworks in Combs-la-Ville were closed down around 1937. In 1945 René Lalique's son, Marc, took over the directorship and artistic direction of the firm after his father's death. The firm exists today under the name Cristallerie Lalique et Cie.

The life work of René Lalique clearly shows that artistic genius eludes the style of a given period. His designs anticipate, long before the First World War, the stylistic features of the Art Deco of the twenties, while in his later works the characteristics of Art Nouveau are clearly manifest. See also Documentation.

162 *Hanging lamp*
Bowl-shaped lamp in opaline
with a design of apples and
leaves.
1925
Sign. R. Lalique, France
∅: 37 cm

163 *Hanging lamp*
Half-sphere in opaline, blown in a
mould, with a bluish gleam
reminiscent of moonstone.
Design of dahlias.
1925
Sign. R. Lalique, France
∅: 30 cm
Ill. *Encyclopédie des Arts
Décoratifs* (Paris, 1925), Vol. V, Pl.
XXIV

164 *Table-lamp*
Milky-white glass cast in a mould,
with a flower design. Base of
hammered wrought iron.
Sign. E. Brandt (Base)
Sign. R. LALIQUE (Shade)
H: 36 cm   Ø: 16 cm

165 *Table-lamp*
White milk glass with a polished
relief design of caryatids.
According to information given
by Miss Marie-Claude Lalique,
made around 1920
Sign. R. LALIQUE
H: 33 cm   W: 22 cm

François-Raoul Larche

Born near Bordeaux in 1860, died in Paris in 1912. Larche's illuminated, gilded-bronze statue, *La Lampe Loie Fuller*, brought him world fame. In two different versions and sizes, it is the centrepiece of many collections today.

Larche came from an ordinary working-class family, but he was, nevertheless, able to study at the Académie des Beaux-Arts in Paris. He was influenced, like Maurice Bouval, by the teacher-sculptor, Alexandre Falguière. Larche exhibited regularly from 1884 until 1911 at the Salon. His main works include *The Storm* (a bronze group in the Grand Palais), *The Seine and its Tributaries*(a fountain-group in the Champs Elysées), and the sculpture, which exists in both marble and cast bronze,*The 12 year-old Jesus in the Temple.*

His best-known work, however, is the lamp cast by Siot-Decauville, depicting the dancer Loie Fuller. Her family name was Marie Louise Fuller. She was born near Chigago (Fullensburg) in 1862 and died in 1928. "La Fuller" became world famous for her dancing with flowing veils and special lighting effects. Toulouse-Lautrec painted her repeatedly. Other artists, such as Pierre Roche, were inspired by Larche's lamp to produce a personal interpretation of the subject.

166   *Decorative lamp*
Illuminated gilt-bronze sculpture
of the dancer Loie Fuller.
Sign. R. Larche
H: 47.5 cm   Ø: 21 cm

Jacques Le Chevalier

Born in Paris in 1896. He was particularly interested in the art of glassmaking and studied at the Ecole Nationale des Arts Décoratifs. A member of the Société des Artistes Décorateurs, he founded, with R. Mallet-Stevens, R. Herbst, and P. Chareau, the Union des Artistes Modernes in 1930. He collaborated with Louis Barillet from 1928 until 1945, and exhibited at the Salon des Indépendants and at the Salon d'Automne. He distinguished himself in many different areas: painting, woodcuts, but above all in the production of lamps. The lamps he produced in collaboration with Raymond Koechlin are particularly original. After 1945 he moved to Fonteney-aux-Roses, where he furnished his own workshop.

167 *Wall-light*
Chromium-plated metal, aluminium and Bakelite.
~ 1928
Sign. Le Chevalier
H: 29.5 cm   Ø: 31 cm

168 *Table-lamp*
Aluminium and Bakelite.
1930
Sign. Le Chevalier
H: 27 cm   W: 25 cm

Pierre Legrain

Born in Levallois-Perret in 1889, died in Paris in 1929. He grew up in an enlightened family milieu: his Belgian mother and French industrialist father early on recognized and encouraged his artistic leanings. He was already producing drawings and caricatures as a boy and was soon discovered by Paul Iribe, the caricaturist and designer, who employed him after 1908. Iribe encouraged Legrain's first attempts at interior design and also introduced him to the Parisian couturier Jacques Doucet, who later became his sponsor. When Iribe travelled to the United States in 1914, Legrain became self-employed, at first without success. In 1917 Jacques Doucet offered him a contract: to rebind the fashion designer's library for a fee of 300 francs a month. Legrain had never designed a book binding before, but nevertheless mastered the art and designed the bindings for 365 volumes. He constantly had to battle against ill health, but despite this, he had great success in 1920 with an exhibition at the Salon des Decorateurs and subsequently became a founder member of the UAM (Union des Artistes Modernes) together with the architect Pierre Chareau, the goldsmith Raymond Templier and the painter Etienne Cournault, all famous in their respective fields.

Legrain frequently tried to commercialize his talents. He opened various boutiques in Paris, but such ventures were short-lived. Legrain was only really interested in original creative work and always gave his best to the increasing number of commissions he received. His work on Paul Meyer's house, for example, was acclaimed by the art critics: the dismal entrance hall was utterly transformed into a fairytale world, in which ceiling, walls and floor were all flooded with light.

Small-scale designing also interested him. He designed cigarette packets for Lucky Strike and Camel, camera cases for Kodak, and the famous black and white bodywork for the Delage car. His sources of inspiration were Cubism, African art and Egypt. He had a preference for beautiful materials which he put together in playful combinations: lacquer-work with leather or chrome, for example. He also used glass and metal with deceptive delicacy, stretching their effects to the limit, as in the famous piano for Pleyel which has been described as the work of a magician. When he died in 1929, a contemporary wrote: "Pierre Legrain is dead. That is a catastrophy for French art."

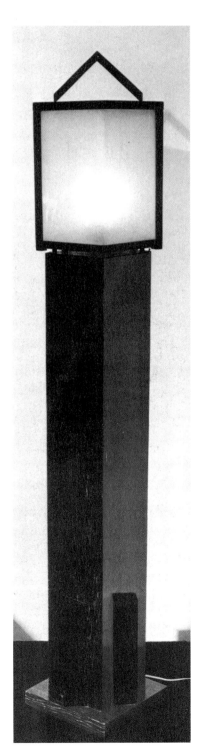

169 *Floor-lamp*
Wood, milk glass and metal with folding handle.
1925
H: 135 cm   Ø: 24 cm

Legras & Cie

Verreries et Cristalleries de St Denis. Bottle-glass works and refinery for the production of both functional and ornamental glassware.
Named after the glassmaker Auguste J.F. Legras in 1864. Alongside Stumpf, Touvier, Violett & Cie, the firm developed into one of the most important factories for the manufacture of tumbler- and bottle-glass, as well as for a wide range of fantasy articles. Around 1900 the works in La Plaine-Saint-Denis and in Pantin were under the direction of François-Théodore Legras, after 1909 under Charles Legras. At the turn of the century they were producing etched cased glass with colourful flower and landscape designs, often with an additional application of enamel painting. Until 1908 they worked on vases and glass reliefs after designs by Lalique. The firm was discontinued in 1914; it started up again after the First World War under the name of Verreries et Cristalleries de St Denis et de Pantin Réunies. Important exhibitions at which the firm was represented include: the 1888 World Exhibition in Barcelona (gold medal, Knighthood of the Legion of Honour); 1889 World Exhibition in Paris (Grand Prix); 1900 World Exhibition in Paris (Grand Prix); 1908 "Exposition Franco-Britannique" in London; 1910 "La Verrerie et la Cristallerie Artistiques" in Paris; and the 1911 International Exhibition in Turin.

170 *Table-lamp*
Multiple cased glass, etched and engraved with a design of budding twigs. Colours: green, gold, yellow, brown. Shade and base both illuminated.
Sign. Legras
H: 38 cm ⌀: 15 cm

Jules-Emile Leleu

Born in Boulogne-sur-Mer in 1883, died in Paris in 1961. He was a pupil of Théophile Deman. At scarcely twenty years of age he set up his own cabinet-making workshop. At first he remained true to the traditions of the eighteenth century, but as early as 1922 he began to produce totally original work. His conception of interior design included every thing, down to the most minor detail. After 1922 he exhibited in various Salons: the Salon des Artistes Decorateurs, Salon d'Automne and Tuileries. He became known to a wider public at the "Arts Décoratifs et Industriels Modernes" Exhibition in 1925, where he showed a salon and a music room for a French embassy. This made his name as *the* interior designer of embassies and luxury liners. His lamps and chandeliers are rare and much sought after. See also Documentation.

171   *Table-lamp*
Base of patinated bronze; shade of beaten brass with gem insets. The geometrical valance is composed of glass beads.
Sign. Leleu
H: 53 cm   ∅: 30 cm

Louis Majorelle

Born in Toul in 1859, died in Nancy in 1926. In 1877 he studied at the Academy in Paris and in 1879 took over his father's ceramic works and furniture workshops in Nancy. After 1900 he worked with Antonin Daum, for whom he made the frames and bases used in his lamps and vases. Majorelle is best known for his pieces of furniture with floral decorative elements. He was an important representative of the Ecole de Nancy.

172   *Hanging lamp*
Daum-glass bowl with coloured powder inclusions, suspended on chains from a canopy composed of three large bronze dragonflies with opaline eyes. Three shades, also of Daum glass, hang from three extended arms.
1898
Bronze frame: Louis Majorelle; glass sign. Daum
H: 90 cm

173 *Hanging lamp*
Elaborate bronze mount, with
three six-sided shades directed
outwards and, hanging lower, a
bowl-shaped glass dish with
inclusions of coloured powder.
Sign. Majorelle (Bronze)
Sign. Daum/Nancy (Glass)
H: 90 cm   Ø: 50 cm

174 *Table-lamp*
The florally decorated bronze
base carries three yellow flowers
made of *pâte-de-verre* glass.
Sign. Daum/Nancy (Glass)
Sign. Majorelle (Bronze)
H: 82 cm   W: 36 cm

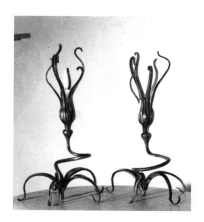

175 *Small table-lamp*
A bronze base supports a yellow dome which has applied beetles. Under the dome is a collar-shaped bronze mount with an abstract floral motif.
Sign. Daum Nancy (Glass)
Sign. Majorelle (Bronze)
H: 30 cm   Ø: 9 cm

177 *Pair of candlesticks*
Wrought iron.
~ 1900
Attributed to Louis Majorelle
H: 34 cm

176 *Table-lamp*
Floral, gilt-bronze base, carries a bud (not lit) and an illuminated flower made of Daum *pâte-de-verre* glass.
~ 1900
Sign. Daum/Nancy (Glass)
Sign. Majorelle (Bronze)
H: 60 cm   Ø: 14 cm

Robert Mallet-Stevens

(1886-1945). As architect, interior decorator and furniture designer, he became known to a wide public through his exhibition of a music room at the Salon d'Automne in 1913. For his interior architectural work he used materials such as steel, chrome and aluminium, sometimes painted to achieve the effect of wood. The years 1923-26 saw the production of three of Mallet-Stevens' major works. In 1923 he drew up the plans for the Vicomte de Noailles' villa in Hyères (Côte d'Azur), a project in which he had completely free rein to put his architectural theories into practice. He designed the sets for Marcel Herbier's well-known film *L'Inhumaine*. The film is watched by connoisseurs today, not only for the production but also for the quality of its sets. With P. Chareau, P. Follot and Süe & Mare, he designed the reception hall for the French Government at the "Exposition des Arts Décoratifs et Industriels Modernes" in 1925. This was Mallet-Stevens' most important period. He joined Van Doesburg and the De Stijl group and worked with a number of famous artists: Laurens, Brancusi, Lipschitz, Delaunay and Leger. His most brilliant creations include: the Château de Mézy in Paris for Paul Poirot in 1924 (Poirot himself never lived there, but the actress Elvire Popesco did, and Max Jacob also made a famous short film there); the building for the Société Alfa-Romeo in the rue Marbeuf in Paris; and the Tourist Pavilion at the Paris exhibition "Arts Décoratifs et Industriels Modernes" in 1925. In 1928 he built the Casino de Saint Jean-de-Luz in southern France. He was the director of the Ecole des Beaux-Arts in Lille from 1936 to 1937. His creative activity ended before the outbreak of war in 1939. He died in 1945 at number 12, rue Mallet-Stevens, the street which bore his name while he was still alive and which was perhaps his greatest masterpiece.
See Documentation.

Charles Martin

Born in Montpellier in 1848, died in 1934. Martin worked in the course of his life as an illustrator and a designer of both *objets d'art* and interiors. Between 1912 and 1925 he worked for a number of well-known French magazines: *Vogue, La Gazette du Bon Ton* and *Le Rire*, and also for *Harper's Bazar*. He also made a name for himself at this time as a stage designer. He continued to design wallpapers, fabrics, furniture and lamps throughout his life.

178 *Floor-lamp*
Chromium-plated metal with
universal joint.
~ 1930
H: 180 cm

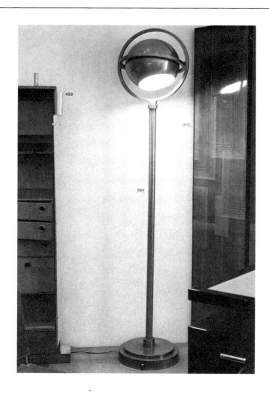

Clément Massier

Born and died in Vallauris, Golfe Juan (1845-1917), the son of a family of potters. Towards 1883, he took over his father's (Jérome Massier) faïence works, which had been producing both utility and decorative ware since 1872. From 1887 to 1895 he collaborated with the painter Lucien Lévi Dhurmer. In 1887 he began working with metal lustres. His earliest known piece is dated 1888.

He showed at many exhibitions, including: 8th "Union Centrale" Exhibition in Paris (1884); 9th "Union Centrale" Exhibition in Paris (1887);

Paris World Exhibition of 1889 (won a gold medal); Salon SNBA in Paris (1891 and 1892).

179 *Lamp*
Base for a petroleum lamp from a model by James Vibert. Manufactured by Clément Massier. Ceramic with greenish blue lustre glaze.
~ 1885
Sign. C. M., with paper label "726"
H: 49 cm (Base)
Ill. *Art et Décoration*, VI (1899), p. 186

180 *Lamp*
A ceramic shaft with a greenish blue lustre glaze on a bronze plate; bronze frame at the top supporting a Tiffany-glass dome, which has a bronze finial.
Sign. Tiffany (Bronze)
Sign. C. Massier (Base)
H: 88 cm   ∅: 21 cm (Dome)

Muller-Frères

The brothers Eugène and Désiré Muller worked with Emile Gallé in Nancy and in around 1910 founded a glass factory in Lunéville. Eugène Muller had already begun manufacturing art glass fifteen years earlier in Croismare, near Lunéville. The Croismare glassworks were amalgamated with the Lunéville factory and up until 1933 were responsible for the production of cased glass with etched or engraved floral motifs and opaque layers of multicoloured powder.

181 *Hanging lamp*
Wrought-iron frame and fixtures, with an abstract design. Two sets of three shades, above and below, and hanging in the centre at the bottom a bowl-shaped shade. Glass coloured with yellow, blue and violet powder. The iron mount is by E. Brandt.
~ 1912
Sign. Muller-Frères, Lunéville (Glass parts)
H: 100 cm   Ø: 90 cm

184 *Table-lamp*
Wrought-iron base with vine leaves and grapes, carrying two shades made of multiple cased glass. Design: various stylized flowers and leaves. Colours: yellow, green, brown, blue.
Sign. Muller-Frères, Lunéville (Glass)
H: 51 cm   Ø: 8 cm

182 *Table-lamp*
Colourless glass with blue spots. Decorated wrought-iron mount.
~1918
Sign. Muller-Frères. Marked: LES ARTS RÉUNIS
H: 45 cm   Ø: 14 cm

183 *Table-lamp*
Cased glass coloured with powder and etched and partly engraved with a floral design. Colours: green, blue, brown, yellow. Shade and base both illuminated.

~ 1910
Sign. Muller-Frères, Lunéville
H: 40 cm   Ø: 19 cm

185 *Small decorative lamp*
Bronze snail on a marble base.
The glass shell, coloured with
oxide inclusions, has been blown
into the bronze frame.
Sign. Chapelle, Nancy (Bronze)
Sign. Muller-Frères (Glass)
L: 34 cm   Ø: 15 cm
Lit. Victor Arwas, *Glass Art
Nouveau to Art Deco*, p. 152

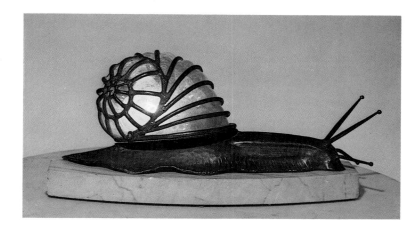

187 *Table-lamp*
Conical shade on a thick glass
base in an iron frame. Shade and
base are cased glass, both
illuminated. The design
represents a landscape with
trees, grass and a lake. Colours:
red, brown, white.
~ 1913
Sign. Muller-Frères, Lunéville
H: 33 cm   Ø: 26 cm

188 *Ceiling-lamp*
Cased glass in yellow and blue,
etched and engraved with a
design of blue anemones.
1910
Sign. Muller-Frères, Lunéville
Ø: 40 cm

189 *Table-lamp*
Multiple cased glass in the base;
single-overlay shade. Both
illuminated. Design: poppy
flowers. Colours: blue, yellow,
green, white.
~ 1912
Sign. Muller-Frères, Lunéville
H: 33 cm   Ø: 16 cm

186 *Table-lamp*
Glass with several overlays. Red
spots and floral design, with
yellow parrots. Colours: red,
yellow, black.
~ 1912
Sign. Muller-Frères, Lunéville
H: 50 cm   Ø: 25 cm

Jean Perzel

Born in Bruck (Austria) in 1892. He was trained as a glass-painter in Munich, travelled on foot across Europe and arrived in Paris in 1910. From 1911 to 1914 he worked as a glass-painter in Algiers. After the First World War he specialized in interior lighting.

He worked with Gruber for a few years and after 1923 devoted himself entirely to designing and manufacturing lamps. At the competition organized by the Salon des Décorateurs in 1928 he received the first prize for decorative lighting. His works were regularly exhibited at the Salon d'Automne, the Salon des Décorateurs and the Société Nationale des Beaux-Arts. In terms of functional conception and decorative construction, Perzel's lamps are perfect. He designed a whole variety of unusual bases and originated a glass of the purest white which was cut in his own studio. What surprises one most with Perzel is the very modernity of his lamps, conceived as they were between 1925 and 1930. Their direct and functional character reveals a great understanding of materials and the purity of the form and the austerity of the materials create an effect of refined elegance.

The lamps exhibited at that time in the rue de la Cité Universitaire 3, in the 14th Arrondissement of Paris, are still fashionable today.

His major works are considered to be: the entire interior lighting of the Palace of the United Nations building in Geneva (following an international competition); the light fittings for the Luxembourg cathedral; the interior lighting for the Henry Ford building in Detroit, USA; the interior decoration for the *Normandie* liner; the designs for the Maharajah's residence in Indor (India), the Cour Royale in Belgium and the Institut Français in London; the interior lighting of the new railway station in Mulhouse (1934); the design of the Emperor of Annam's residence in Dalat, and the Royal Chitralada Palace (the King of Siam's residence in Bangkok).

See also Documentation.

190 *Table-lamp*
Metal lacquered in an ivory colour.
1925
Sign. Perzel
H: 34 cm   Ø: 16 cm

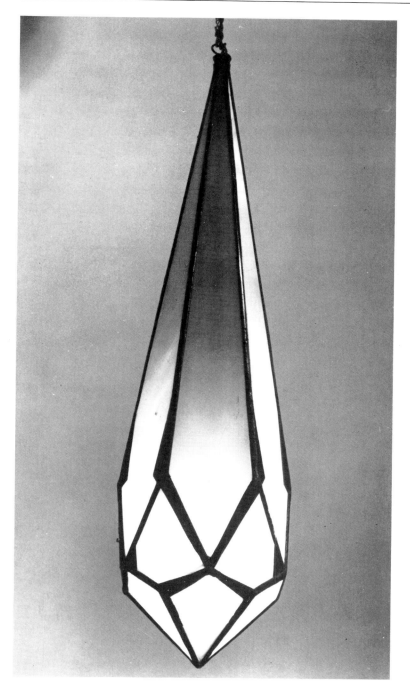

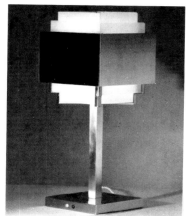

192 *Writing-desk lamp*
Milky glass and chromium-plated metal.
1925
Sign. Perzel
H: 43 cm   Ø: 24 cm (diagonal)

193 *Writing-desk lamp*
Bronze, chromium-plated metal and milky glass.
1924
H: 38 cm   Ø: 22 cm

191 *Hanging lamp*
Milky glass set in a lead frame.
1924
Sign. Perzel
H: 95 cm   Ø: 23 cm

194 *Pair of wall-lights*
Smooth and rough milk glass on a chromed-metal base.
~ 1926
Sign. Jean Perzel
H: 36 cm

Eugène Printz

Designer and decorator. Biographical details not known.

195 *Floor-lamp*
Oxidized brass and black
lacquered wood.
1928
H: 179 cm   Ø: 54 cm

Jean E. Puiforcat

Born and died in Paris (1867-1945). French sculptor and goldsmith. He learned his trade with his father, developing his own style after 1922. At the Art Deco exhibition in 1925 he exhibited a number of valuable gold objects richly decorated with other materials. He also made a name for himself by combining in his silver creations precious materials such as ivory, ebony, jade, lapis lazuli and crystal. The official catalogue of the 1925 Art Deco exhibition in Paris described Puiforcat as one of the "great initiators of modern functionalism". He was the most important goldsmith working in the Art Deco style in the 1920s.

196   *Pair of candlesticks*
Silver-plated, in a severe geometrical style. Marked: E. P. with candlestick symbol and the right profile of a head.
1925
Sign. J. Puiforcat
H: 6 cm   W: 23 cm

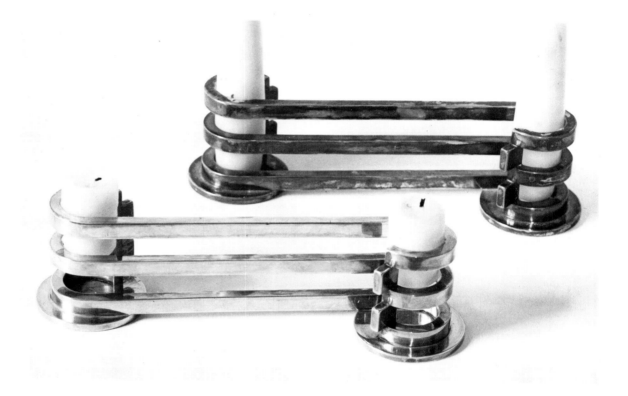

Armand-Albert Rateau

Born in Paris in 1882. His artistic abilities were apparent at an early age. He learned to draw and to sculpt in wood at the Ecole Boulle. When he was hardly sixteen years old he rented a studio and worked for various interior designers, in particular Georges Hoentschel (1855-1915), from whom he learnt a great deal. From 1905 to 1914 he directed the interior-design studios at the well-known Maison Alavoine. He became self-employed after the First World War. Amongst his customers was the famous milliner Jeanne Lanvin, from whom he received numerous commissions, including the designs for her house in the rue Barbet de Vony in Paris, later unfortunately destroyed. Prince Louis de Polignac, Jeanne Lanvin's grandson, donated the furniture and *objets d'art* from this house to the Musée des Arts Décoratifs in Paris. Rateau also designed the boutique Lanvin Sport for Mme Lanvin. The Théâtre Dauneau was also executed to his designs between 1920 and 1925.

For the American George Blumenthal he designed the interiors of a palace near Grasse and houses in Paris and New York. He designed the bathroom for the Duchess of Alba in the Palais Liria in Madrid between 1925 and 1926 and the Baroness Rothschild's Paris house. Rateau was a definite outsider when it came to artists' groups and exhibitions in the Salons: he took no part in either. He had a predilection for lighting and his artistic leanings were towards ancient and Eastern art. He preferred working in heavy, solid woods like oak, to which he would apply gold or silver lacquer. He is also known for works in burnished metal, which he produced with the help of the sculptor Paul Plumet. All Rateau's creations are valued for their elegance and luxurious quality.

197   *Two floor-lamps*
Burnished metal. The first lamp has birds' (geese?) heads extending from an abstract design of daisies. The second has lowered birds' heads, three of which have a snake in their beaks, in front of an abstract design. Both lamps were designed for Jeanne Lanvin and were shown at the Paris exhibition "Arts Décoratifs et Industriels Modernes".
1921
H: ~ 2.30 m

Emile Robert

Born and died in Mehun-sur-Yèvre (1860-1924). It was in this charming little market town near Bourges that Emile Robert learnt his trade from a reputable craftsman named Larchevêque. His preferred medium was iron and Robert was soon to become one of the leading craftsmen responsible for the reintroduction of this material into nineteenth-century France. In his work and in the many articles that he wrote he showed himself to be "a peculiarly creative and honest artist", who succeeded in combining "the functional with the ingenious and imaginative". Whether for a piece of lattice-work or for a hanging lamp, he always used forged and beaten iron. His preference was for fragile motifs such as cornflowers and poppies, executed nevertheless in strong, clear lines.

198 *Hanging lamp*
Glass cast in a mould. Frame of chromium-plated metal.
~ 1928
Sign. E. Robert
∅: 52 cm

Robj

A French dealer who specialized in the applied arts of the twenties and thirties. He commissioned various craftsmen to make small porcelain figures, ink-pots, ashtrays, pots, cigarette-boxes, bottles, smoke consumers, and lamps, to which his signature was then applied.

Between 1920 and 1930 he organized an annual design competition, and gave some of the winning designs to the Sèvres firm to produce in a limited edition. Some works show the name of the designer next to the signature Robj/Paris, Made in France.

199 *Small table-lamp*
Crystal glass cast in a mould, with a design of kneeling and seated female nudes. Base of hammered wrought iron.
Sign. ROBJ, PARIS (Shade and base)
H: 14 cm   Ø: 12 cm

Emile-Jacques Ruhlmann

Born and died in Paris (1879-1933). Just as Reisener was the sole representative of the art of cabinet-making in the time of Louis XVI, so the name of Ruhlmann is associated with a particular conception of Art Deco furniture in France – one that involves the highest degree of quality, elegance and technical skill. Ruhlmann exhibited for the first time in 1913 at the Salon d'Automne and immediately earned himself a name as the creator of luxury furniture. After the First World War he founded the firm of Ruhlmann and Laurent, which manufactured furniture and objects after his designs until his death. Encouraged by the work of the *ébénistes* (workers in ebony) he experimented with rare woods such as amboina, amaranth, violet-wood and Macassar ebony, also inlays of ivory and other rare materials like marocain and sharkskin. His simple, elegant, discreetly curving shapes and the slender legs characteristic of his furniture after 1913 are in the tradition of the eighteenth century.

At the Art Deco exhibition of 1925 he showed *L'Hotel du Collectionneur*, put together with the help of the architect Pierre Patout and a group of artists and craftsmen: Joseph Bernard, Bourdelle, Despiau, Pompon, Léon Jallot, Francis Jourdain, Rapin, Jean Puiforcat, Brandt, Decoeur, Lenoble, Dunand, Décorchement, Legrain and Bastard.

In the last years of his life he began to use chromium-plated metal and silver in the construction and decoration of his furniture and set about producing functional furniture made of box shapes placed one on top of the other. Ruhlmann was primarily a craftsman, but he was also interested in other aspects of furnishing; with the help of Stephan he produced designs for fabrics and wallpapers. His large patterns with flowers or birds either kept to dull colours or were painted in monochrome whereby Ruhlmann avoided using classic damask. He also created a number of lamps and wall-brackets.

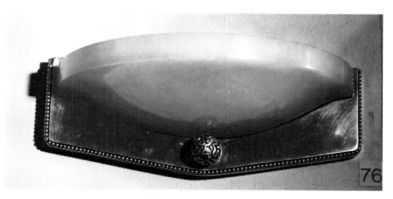

200   *Table-lamp*
Coloured crystal glass in the shape of a vase. Base of gilded bronze. Design: Ruhlmann.
~ 1926
H: 43 cm   ∅: 24 cm

201   *Wall-bracket*
Polished bronze, with a silver design. Shade of polished alabaster.
1921
Shade: 34 x 17 cm
Bronze: 36 x 13 cm

202   *Wall-bracket*
Purse-shaped. Chased bronze with a chrome design; alabaster shade.
1923
Shade: 36 x 64 cm
Bronze: 26 x 14 cm

Maurius-Ernest Sabino

Born in Paris in 1878, year of death unknown. A craftsman in glass, he studied at the Ecole Nationale des Arts Décoratifs and the Ecole Nationale des Beaux-Arts in Paris. After 1913 he designed scent-bottles, vases and lighting, and also furniture and glass parts for use in architecture, which were produced as single items and also in series by the glassworks in Romilly-sur-Andelle and Bagnolet, Seine, and later in Noisy-le-Sec. From about 1930 Sabino had his own sales- and showrooms in Paris. Important exhibitions to which he contributed were: the "Arts Décoratifs et Industriels Modernes" in Paris (1925); the 1927 and 1928 Salon exhibitions in Paris, and the 1930 World Exhibition in Liège. See also Documentation.

203 *Wall-light*
Colourless Sabino glass with fruit
and leaves in relief; hammered
wrought-iron frame.
~ 1925
H: 24.5 cm   W: 26.5 cm

204 *Table-lamp*
Chrome.
1925
Sign. Sabino Paris
H: 32 cm   Ø: 20 cm

205 *Floor-lamp*
Chromed metal with richly
decorated moulded glass, stained
yellow and blue.
1924
H: 92 cm   Ø: 20 cm

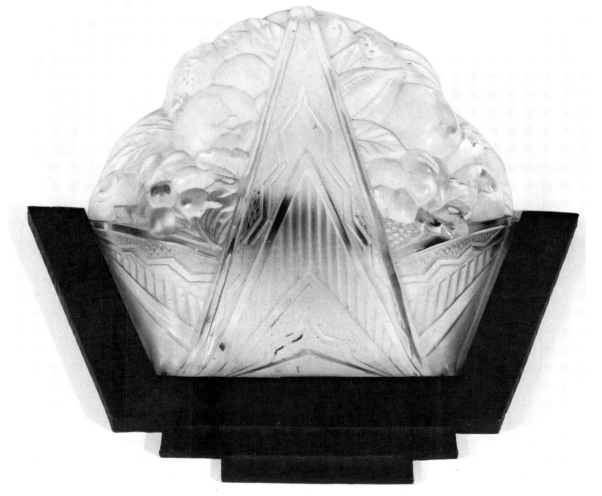

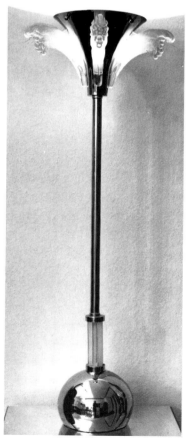

Charles Schneider

(1881-1962). He and his brother Ernest founded the Cristallerie Schneider in Epinay-sur-Seine in 1913. Ernest took over the business side and Charles became artistic director of the firm. As a young man he attended the Ecole des Beaux-Arts in Nancy, and afterwards worked there as a designer for Gallé and the Daum Brothers. Under his influence the Cristallerie Schneider attained increasing artistic importance. Besides art glass of all kinds, lamps and candlesticks were also produced. In the twenties the firm made crystal and cased glass with stylized geometric decorations under the name *le verre français*. Instead of the Schneider signature one sometimes finds an inlaid thread of red, white and blue glass. Those pieces which are signed "Charder", an abbreviation of *Char*les and Schnei*der*, are particutarly sought after today.

207 *Table-lamp*
Glass shade with pink powder inclusions. The base and mount are gilded bronze. Mistletoe design on the foot; the mount has three dragonflies. Two glass shades.
Sign. Schneider
H: 55.5 cm   Ø: 39.5 cm

208 *Table-lamp*
Spherical base with wrought-iron mount. Mushroom-shaped shade with multicoloured powder inclusions. Etched surface. Shade and base both illuminated.
~ 1920
Sign. Schneider
H: 43 cm   Ø: 24 cm

206 *Decorative lamp*
Patinated bronze in the shape of a pheasant. The body is made of blown glass with powder inclusions.
~ 1908
Bronze sign. Chapelle, Nancy
Glass: Sign. Schneider
H: 45 cm (Tail)
W: 55 cm

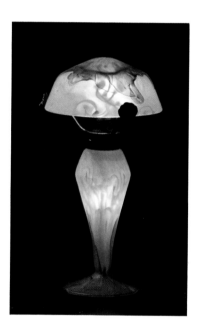

209 *Table-lamp*
Base and shade of glass with inclusions of variously coloured powder and oxides which run in a veil-like pattern over the shade. Wrought-iron frame.
~ 1914
Sign. Schneider
H: 36 cm   Ø: 17.5 cm

210 *Candlestick*
Glass nozzle coloured with purple and yellow powder. Base with three glass balls the same colour as the nozzle, and carved beech leaves.
~ 1910
Etched sign. on base: Schneider, France
H: 28 cm

Pierre Selmersheim

Dates unknown. Interior designer. He worked with his brother Tony. Maurice Dufrène often quotes him, with regard to furniture and seating, in the series of articles he wrote for the magazine *Art et Décoration* (e. g., Vol. XXXIV (1913), pp. 81-92), and emphasizes the rare materials the two brothers chose for their furniture. Pierre Selmersheim was vice-president of the Société des Artistes Décorateurs in 1913. Lamps or candlesticks by him are rare.

211 *Candlestick*
Two-branched. Silvered brass.
1900
Design: Pierre Selmersheim
H: 26 cm   W: 24 cm
Ill. *Art et Décoration, X (1901),
p. 24*

Manufacture Nationale Sèvres

The firm, transferred in 1756 from Vincennes to Sèvres, worked exclusively after 1759 under the auspices of the king. It was the leading porcelain firm of the eighteenth century and soon gave rise to competition from smaller Parisian manufacturers.

Throughout the nineteenth century Sèvres was a state firm – and it remains so today – serving the needs of monarchy and republic in turn, but always receptive to the latest styles and techniques. Other smaller, private firms exist alongside the state one at Sèvres.

212 *Floor-lamp*
An illuminated Sèvres vase in
enamelled porcelain with a
flower composition. Gilt-bronze
base.
1928
Marked inside: SÈVRES
Manufacture Nationale France
and signed near the foot: Ch. Fritz
d'ap. Beaumont
H: 50 cm

213 *Decorative lamp*
Represents a lighted fountain.
The engraved design covers the
inverted dome (inside and
outside), base and small shade.
Enamelled porcelain; the fittings
are bronze.
1925
Sign. S. SÈVRES
MANUFACTURE, b, (scratched)
PN N
30 3 C
H: 143 cm   ∅: 66 cm

Raymond Subes

(1893-1970). He studied at the Ecole Boulle, principally metalwork, and afterwards at the Ecole des Arts Décoratifs. He worked for three years in Emile Robert's studio, where he acquired great technical expertise, and in 1919 took over as artistic director of the Borderel and Robert workshops. He combined in his work traditional wrought-iron techniques with modern methods. His conception of ironworking was based on two ideas: the architectural function of wrought iron and its functional application. He was not afraid of combining various materials.
At the Paris Exhibition of 1925, apart from works in wrought iron such as lattices and stair-railings, he exhibited work produced in collaboration with Ruhlmann: the furnishings for a library made of metal with surfaces of beaten and lacquered plate. With Porteneuve he later produced chromium-plated metal furniture, and contributed to the production of metal for bridges. Araund 1920 he began designing lamps. He made many light fittings, candlesticks, candelabra, wall-brackets and ceiling lights: "Splendid chandeliers or discreet lanterns, in which the iron was interlaced or branching, massed or worked into delicate acanthus leaves to achieve the subtlest effects" (*La Ferronerie Moderne*). See Documentation.

Louis Marie L. Süe

Born in Bordeaux in 1875. Year of death unknown. French architect, painter and interior designer. In 1901 he had his first exhibition at the Indépendants. In 1919 he founded with André Mare the Compagnie des Arts Français on the corner of the Faubourg Saint Honoré and l'Avenue Matignon. The Compagnie was soon to count among its members: Paul Véra, Jaulmes, R. Desvallières, Ch. Dufresne, Segonzac and Maurice Marinot. All the aspects of interior design were represented there: decoration, furniture, fabrics, ceramics, glass, bronzes, lamps, etc. 1921 saw the publication of Süe et Mare's first manifesto, for which Paul Valéry wrote a passage. Later Louis Süe also designed the fittings for the Metropolitan Museum in New York. Süe received the French National Prize in 1957.
See Documentation.

Süe & Mare

Producers of exclusive furniture, carpets and textiles, also known under the name Compagnie des Arts Français. Louis Süe founded the firm in 1919 together with André Mare (1887-1932). Contemporary literature at the beginning of the twenties depicts numerous lamps and wall-brackets designed by Süe & Mare.
See Documentation.

Almaric-V. Walter

Born in Sèvres in 1859, died in Nancy in 1942. Walter was apprenticed at the state firm of Sèvres. His first *pâte-de-verre* objects were made in collaboration with Gabriel Lévy. He showed at the Paris Salon for the first time in 1903: figurines, medallions and vases made of opal *pâte-de-verre*. In 1908 he joined Daum Frères in Nancy. There he created animal statues such as mice, frogs, chameleons, snails and crabs, made of *pâte-de-verre*, from designs and drawings by H. Bergé. He stayed with Daum until 1914. After the First World War, in 1919, he opened his own studio for the production of *pâte-de-verre*, in Nancy, employing about twenty workers and working to designs by Jules Chéret, Cayette and Descomps, among others.

214 *Table-lamp*
Shade in *pâte-de-verre*, folded together like a handkerchief. The glass is light blue merging into dark blue with six large patches of powder inclusions ranging from orange to fiery red and spreading net-like over the shade. Base and shaft are wrought iron. The base has a design of ginkgo leaves and fruit.
~ 1919
Sign. Walter, Nancy
H: 44 cm   Ø: 17.5 cm

215 *Decorative lamp*
Pâte-de-verre, representing a female nude standing in water in front of stylized reeds and a rising sun. Wrought-iron frame.
~ 1925
Sign. A. WALTER NANCY
H: 28 cm

216 *Decorative lamp*
Opaline with flying swans, their
bodies in high relief, water and
fishes.
∼ 1926
Sign. Verlys, France
H: 16 cm

219 *Decorative lamp*
Gilt bronze, representing a nude
girl, leaves and flowers, mounted
on a marble base.
∼ 1900
H: 27 cm

217 *Ceiling-lamp*
Moulded glass with relief design
of flowers and abstract motifs.
∼ 1925
H: 47 cm

220 *Decorative lamp*
Gilt bronze, representing a
woman holding a flower over her
head.
∼ 1895
Sign. P. Moreau-Vauthier
H: 42 cm

218 *Decorative lamp*
Girl in a flowing dress holding in
her outstretched arms a flower-
shaped shade. Patinated bronze.
Moulded-glass lampshade.
∼ 1900
Sign. Maxim, Paris
H: 32.7 cm

221 *Decorative lamp*
Highly stylized figure of a girl
rising up from water lily pads and
holding a flower above her head.
Patinated bronze mounted on an
alabaster foot.
∼ 1900
H: 34 cm

222 *Table-lamp*
Base and decoration in hammered, bronzed wrought iron. Dome of colourless moulded glass with flower design.
H: 47 cm   Ø: 15 cm

226 *Table-lamp*
Chromed-metal base with geometrical relief and a mirror surface. The body of the lamp is made of yellowish opaline.
~ 1926
Possibly Sabino, France
H: 33 cm

223 *Decorative lamp*
The elongated foot of an inkwell extends into the figure of a woman clasping the stem of a hydrangea. Gilt bronze; the flower also incorporates pink *pâte-de-verre*.
~ 1898
Foundry mark:
Louchet, Paris
H: 33.5 cm   W: 30 cm

227 *Ceiling-light*
Yellow, gold, pink and white opaline. The glass parts are set in lead in a strictly geometrical arrangement.
~ 1925
H: 55 cm   Ø: 52 cm

224 *Decorative lamp*
Patinated bronze, representing a crane among reeds and marsh flowers.
~ 1925
H: 53 cm

225 *Ceiling-light*
Three gilt-bronze twigs each hold a flower of colourless *pâte-de-verre*.
~ 1895
(Ecole de Nancy)
H: 120 cm   Ø: 85 cm

228 *Floor-lamp*
The base is a combination of wood (painted and lacquered), chromed metal, and glass, standing on a copper ring.
~ 1925
Design: Martell (?)
H: 200 cm   Ø: 50 cm

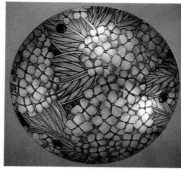

229 *Ceiling-light*
Moulded, stained-glass globe
with an engraved relief design of
flowers and fir twigs. Colours:
red, blue, green, yellow, white.
~ 1929
Sign. Loys Luchg

230 *Small table-lamp*
Milk glass and chromed metal.
1925
Sign. Worth
H: 22 cm   Ø: 14.5 cm

231 *Table-lamp*
Chromed-metal base. Shade of
folded colourless moulded glass.
~ 1926
H: 37 cm   Ø: 20 cm

232 *Table-lamp*
Chromium-plated metal and
milk glass
~ 1925
H: 25 cm

233 *Pair of candlesticks*
Patinated bronze, representing a
cluster of fruit raised above three
ivy leaves.
~ 1910
Sign. Bundeau
H: 29 cm   W: 16.5 cm (Base)

234 *Ceiling-light*
Gilt bronze, representing a
mistletoe branch. Nine light
bulbs represent the berries.
~ 1898
H: 100 cm   W: ~ 90 cm

235 *Hanging lamp*
Described by Simonet Frères as
Les Palmettes. Colourless
moulded-glass dome with sixteen
single parts composing the
wreath-shaped rim which curves
upwards.
1929
Ø: 120 cm
Ill. *Chez Moi* (June/July 1930)
See also Documentation

236 *Table-light*
Horn of Plenty. Oxidized
aluminium with a crystal base.
~ 1925
H: 29 cm   W: 55 cm

237 *Candlestick*
Four-branched, zinc, with a leaf
design on a round base.
1900
Mark: 4467 and cockerel (Gallia-
Métal)
H: 32 cm

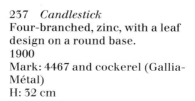

238 *Pair of candlesticks*
Three-branched, representing a
female figure with long hair,
whose body swirls up out of the
round base. Cast bronze, silvered.
1900
Sign. on the base: C. Bonnefond;
stamped: U 3
H: 32.5 cm

Desny

Christian name and particulars unknown.
See also Documentation.

239   *Small table-lamp*
Glass plates, laid one on top of
another, on an aluminium base.
~ 1926
H: 16 cm   ⌀: 16 cm

IV GERMANY

Bauhaus

Walter Gropius founded the Bauhaus – as an art institute and educational centre – by amalgamating the Weimar Art Academies in 1919. The Bauhaus remained in Weimar until 1925, when it moved to Dessau.

The goal of the Bauhaus was "the realization of a modern architecture which, like human nature, embraces the whole of life". It was divided up into classes and groups, and supplemented by workshops. Among those who taught there were: Feininger, Marcks, Itten, Schlemmer, Kandinsky and Moholy-Nagy. When Gropius left in 1928,

Hannes Meyer became the new director. A large police force closed the Bauhaus on 10 April 1933 because it was, according to Hitler, "a cathedral of socialism".

László Moholy-Nagy was director of the metal workshop at the Bauhaus from 1923 to 1928, and as such was particularly interested in the development of modern lamps of simple shape made out of the (then) new materials aluminium and chromium, combined with opaque and matt glass. Among his colleagues were Marianne Brandt and Max Krajewski.

240 *Floor-lamp*
Aluminium and chrome on a round base, with a rounded flat shade in pale-blue matt opaline.
~ 1925
Design: M. Krajewski
H: 147 cm   ∅: 52 cm

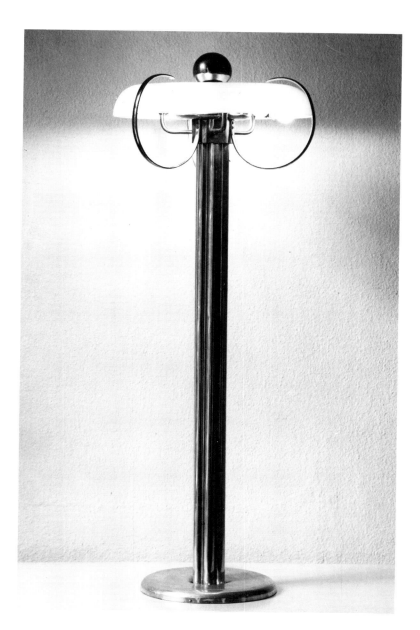

Peter Behrens

Born in Hamburg in 1868, died in Berlin in 1940. He studied painting from 1886 to 1889 at the Karlsruhe Academy and under Ferdinand Brütt in Düsseldorf. He lived in Munich after 1890 and was a founder of the Secession in 1892, and a founder member, in 1898, of the Vereinigte Werkstätten für Kunst im Handwerk (United Workshops for Art in the Handcrafts). Until his appointment to the Artists' Colony in Darmstadt, Behrens was mainly occupied as a painter, commercial artist, and a designer of lettering. His first architectural task was the building of the Behrens family house, for which he also designed the whole of the interior. His versatility in the field of the applied arts laid the foundations for Behrens' later industrial work. During his time in Darmstadt, Behrens took part in the 1900 World Exhibition in Paris, and the 1902 "International Exhibition of Modern and Decorative Art" in Turin, as well as the first Artists' Colony Studio Exhibition in Darmstadt. In the winter of 1902/03 Behrens took the master course at the Bavarian Industrial Museum in Nuremberg. He was director of the School of Arts and Crafts in Düsseldorf (1903-07) and worked as artistic adviser for the AEG in Berlin from 1907. He officiated in 1922-36 as professor and director of the School of Architecture at the Vienna Academy, and in 1936 he ran an architectural workshop at the Academy of Arts in Berlin.

241   *Table-lamp*
Gilded bronze, opalescent glass.
1902
H: 66.5 cm

242   *Hanging lamp*
Four arms. Brass with
transparent opaline globes.
~ 1903
Design: Peter Behrens
H: 105 cm   Ø: 80 cm

Rudolf Bosselt

Born in Perleberg in the district of Potsdam, in 1871, died in Berlin in 1938. From 1885 to 1891 he learned and practised the trade of engraver in a factory producing bronze articles in Berlin. He received his training as a sculptor and medallist at the School of Arts and Crafts in Frankfurt am Main, under the sculptor Wiedemann and the engraver J. Kowarzik, under whose guidance he produced his first plaques. At the same time Bosselt studied anatomy at the Städel Institute. He was a pupil of the sculptor D. P. Puech at the Académie Julian in Paris from 1897 to 1899. He received an honourable mention at the Salon in 1897, and the first prize in a competition for the design of a baptismal medallion organized by the Prussian State, which also brought attention to Bosselt's work in the field of art medallions.

From 1899 to 1903 he was a member of the Artists' Colony in Darmstadt where he produced jewellery, small bronzes and utility metal objects, and especially metal medallions and plaques. He was also writing at this time about the revival of the art of making medallions. In 1900 he took part in the World Exhibition in Paris, and at the first exhibition of the Artists' Colony in 1901 he presented a special showing of his work. He taught at the School of Arts and Crafts in Düsseldorf from 1903 to 1911, and was director of the Schools of Arts and Crafts and Manual Trades in Magdeburg from 1911 to 1925. He directed the School of Arts and Crafts in Braunschweig from 1928 to 1931. From 1931 he lived in Berlin.

243   *Table-lamp*
Partly gilded bronze with coloured stones set on a marble base. The figure holds a circular neon tube.
1901
H: 33 cm

Eduard Foehr

A Stuttgart jeweller, whose work was
particularly prized at the turn of the century.

244 *Candlestick*
Shaped like an iris. Silver.
~ 1899
Designed and made by Eduard
Foehr, Stuttgart
H: 28 cm

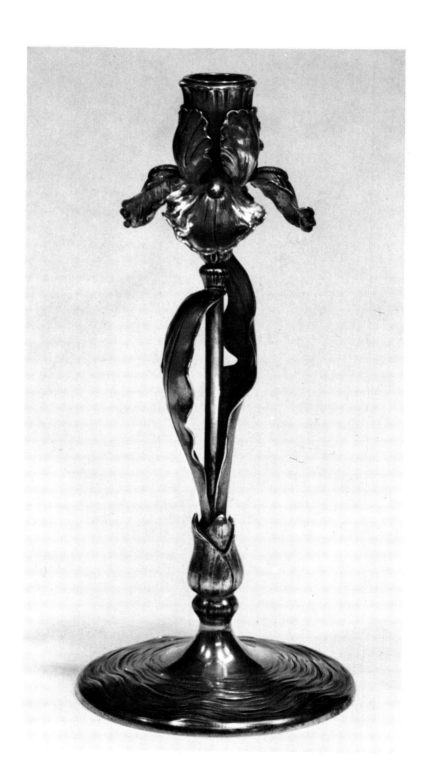

Gerhardi & Cie

Pewter foundry. Founded around 1800. In 1870 it began producing so-called "Britannia Metal" (a pewter alloy). The factory closed down its production during the First World War. Among the artists who worked for the firm were: Joseph Olbrich, Albin Müller and Paul Haustein.

245 *Candlestick*
Two arms; pewter.
~ 1903
Design: Albert Reimann, Berlin
Produced by Gerhardi & Cie,
Lüdenscheid
H: 39 cm

246 *Candlesticks*
Single and double-armed,
decorated with the same stylized
floral design. Pewter.
~ 1900
Produced by Gerhardi & Cie,
Lüdenscheid
H: 28 cm   H: 22 cm

Ludwig Habich

Born in Darmstadt in 1872, died in Jugenheim in 1949. From 1890 to 1892 he was a pupil of the sculptor G. Kaupert at the Städel Institute in Frankfurt am Main. From 1892 to 1895 he studied with the sculptor H. Volz at the Academy in Karlsruhe and with W. v. Rümann at the Munich Academy. At this time he was already designing various monuments. From 1899 to 1906 he was a member of the Artists' Colony in Darmstadt where he also took the sculpture course at Adolf

Beyer's Art School after 1901. During his Darmstadt period, he took part in the Artists' Colony's Exhibitions, as well as in the various shows organized by the Free Society of Darmstadt Artists, of which he was a founder member in 1897. He held the post of Professor of Decorative Sculpture at the Technical High School in Stuttgart from 1906 to 1910, and was afterwards professor at the Stuttgart Academy until 1937. He returned to Darmstadt in 1937.

247 *Bedside table-lamp*
Bronze. The original reflector is missing.
1901
Manufactured by A. Brandstätter, Munich
H: 17.5 cm

Paul Haustein

Born in Chemnitz in 1880, died in Stuttgart in 1944. He attended the Schools of Arts and Crafts in Dresden (1896-97) and Munich (1897-98), and afterwards studied with the painter J. Herterich at the Munich Academy (1898-99). After 1897 he collaborated on the magazine *Jugend* and after 1899 worked as a practical designer in the metal workshops of the Vereinigte Werkstätten für Kunst im Handwerk in Munich. At the same time he worked for J. J. Scharvogel's Munich ceramics firm, for the Seifert light-fittings works in Dresden, and for the silverware factory of Bruckmann Sons in Heilbronn. He was invited to

join the Artists' Colony in Darmstadt in 1903 and took part in their second exhibition in 1904, where he showed various furnished rooms, graphic and applied work. He won a distinction at the World Exhibition in St Louis in the same year. The government of Hessen commissioned him to study the pottery trade in north Hessen, and his designs had a lasting influence on the production of ceramics there. After 1905 he was a teacher, and after 1907 professor in the metal section of the Lehr- und Versuchswerkstätten (Training and Experimental Workshops) of the School of Arts and Crafts in Stuttgart.

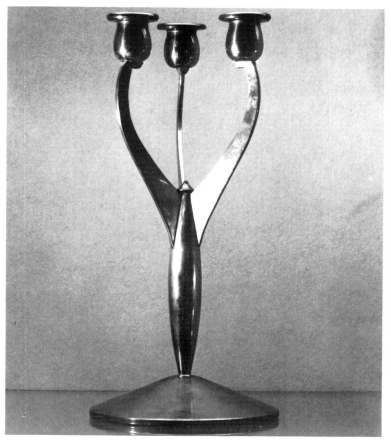

248   *Candlesticks*
Brass, in similar designs.
1902
Design: Paul Haustein
Manufactured by the Vereinigte
Werkstätten für Kunst im
Handwerk, Munich
H: 29 cm   H: 35 cm

249   *Candlestick*
Three-branched. Brass.
1904
Design: Paul Haustein. Made by
A. G. Pöschmann, Dresden
H: 35 cm

J. P. Kayser

Leuconide metalware factory and business in Krefeld-Bockum and Cologne. Manufacturers of pewter.
The pewter foundry was transferred in 1862 from Kaiserswerth to Krefeld-Bockum and in 1885 was enlarged and modernized. The craftsman Engelbert Kayser (1840-1911) set up a studio for decorative pewter in Cologne around 1900, where the designs and models for the foundry were made. The foundry in Krefeld was under the direction of his brother, Johann Peter Kayser. After 1900 the firm took part in international exhibitions. Kayser developed a new way of casting pewter. The so-called "Kayserzinn" consisted of pure pewter with additions of copper and antimony, which gave the polished surfaces a silvery gleam and great stability. The fact that Kayserzinn contained no lead enabled the product to be used for all types of tableware. A clue in dating the pieces may be found in the model numbers which Kayser began marking around 1894/95, starting with the fictitious number 4000. The number 4264 was reached in 1898. The catalogue of 1909 ends the Jugendstil selection with the number 4999.

250 *Candlestick*
Abstract design. A tall, slender
shaft on a round foot. Polished.
1901
Marked: Kayser-Zinn No. 4427
H: 42 cm
Lit. *Kayser-Zinn*,
Helmut Hentrich Collection,
Catalogue of the Museum für
Kunst und Gewerbe,
Hamburg (1974), p. 27,
Ill. No. 56.
Landesmuseum Darmstadt,
Catalogue, p. 221, Ill. No. 249

252 *Candlestick*
For carrying. Abstract floral
design. Pewter.
~ 1902
Sign. KAYSERZINN 4406
H: 9 cm

251 *Candlestick*
Pewter. Leaf-like decoration on
the shaft.
~ 1903
Sign. KAYSERZINN 4465
H: 32 cm

253 *Candlestick*
Pewter. Decorated with berries
and Aron's Rod leaves.
~ 1900
Sign. KAYSERZINN 4279
H: 24.5 cm

254 *Two small oil lamps*
Both in pewter.
Left: out of a hollow base rises a tape-like handle and a quadrangular shaft which tapers towards the top.
1900
Designed by Joseph Maria Olbrich (?)
H: 22.7 cm

Right: on the base and oil reservoir a design of soap plant with fruit pods and stalks.
1900-02
Sign. KAYSERZINN 4439
H: 24 cm

255 *Candlestick*
Combined with an ashtray. Abstract floral design. Polished pewter.
1905
Sign. KAYSERZINN 4607
H: 7 cm   W: 17 cm

258 *Candlestick*
Abstract floral design, polished pewter with two handles.
~ 1902
Sign. KAYSERZINN 4379
H: 6.5 cm   W: 13 cm

256 *Candlestick*
Three-armed. Stylized arrowroot flowers and leaves. Pewter.
1901
Sign. KAYSERZINN 4328
H: 33 cm

259 *Candlestick*
Five-armed. Floral design. Pewter.
1902-04
Design: Hugo Leven
Sign. KAYSERZINN 4486
H: 48.5 cm

257 *Candelabrum*
With a holder for matchsticks and an ashtray. Pewter.
1904-06
Sign. Kayser 4628
H: 25 cm

260 *Candelabrum*
Three-branched. Bats with outstretched wings provide the attachment for the curved arms.
~ 1904
Sign. KAYSERZINN 4506
H: 30.5 cm

261 *Candlestick*
Pewter, decorated with a pattern
of leaves and stems.
~ 1904
Design: Hugo Leven, 1903
Sign. KAYSERZINN 4521
H: 30 cm

262 *Candlestick*
With a handle. Pewter.
~ 1902
Sign. KAYSERZINN 4449
H: 8.5 cm

264 *Candlestick*
Combined with a small dish.
Flower design. Polished pewter.
1900
Sign. KAYSERZINN 4018
H: 5.3 cm   L: 20 cm

263 *Candlestick*
For carrying. Leaf design. Stands
on four round feet. Pewter.
1897
Sign. KAYSERZINN 4457
H: 5 cm

265 *Candlestick*
On a saucer base. Abstract
design. Polished pewter.
1901
Sign. KAYSERZINN 4384
H: 7 cm   L: 26.5 cm

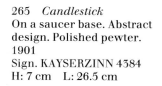

Albin Müller

Born in Dittersbach (Erzgebirge) in 1871, died in Darmstadt in 1943. After training for three years as a joiner with his father, he served as a journeyman after 1890 under various masters and in various furniture works. He worked from 1893 to 1897 as a furniture draughtsman and interior designer in larger furniture works and so earned the money which enabled him to study at the School of Arts and Crafts in Mainz and at the Academy in Dresden. He taught interior design and architecture at the School of Arts and Crafts in Magdeburg from 1900 to 1906. In October 1906 he was invited to join the Artists' Colony in Darmstadt and worked there from

1907 until 1911 as a teacher of interior design in the Grand Duke's training studios. He produced a great many designs for applied art projects and played an essential part in the architectural construction of the Hessen Regional Exhibition in 1908. He was the leading architect of the Artists' Colony after J. M. Olbrich's death, and drew up the plan for the Colony's third exhibition in 1914. Müller received numerous architectural commissions and also published various works on architecture and the applied arts (*Architektur und Raumkunst*, 1909; *Neue Werkkunst*, 1927, etc.).

266 *Small oil-lamp*
Abstract design. Pewter. ~1902
Sign. AM = Albin Müller
Marked: E. Hueck H : 22 cm
The Eduard Hueck pewter foundry was founded in 1814 in Lüdenscheid as a factory and business dealing in iron, steel, and brassware. After 1878 the firm began producing pewter: Britannia Metal (an English pewter alloy), *Edelzinn* and *Silberzinn*. Designers at the turn of the century included: J. M. Olbrich, Peter Behrens and Albin Müller.

268 *Candelabrum*
Five-branched. Cast iron. Before 1904. Marked with a shield with a running stag, "Gesetzlich geschützt ST.W 4013". Manufactured by "Fürstlich Stollbergsches Hüttenamt, Ilsenburg a. H ."
H: 48.3 cm
W: 22.5 cm
World Exhibition St Louis 1904
Lit. *Deutsche Kunst und Dekoration* (1904), p. 496

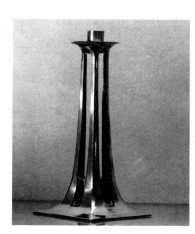

267 *Candlestick*
Silvered brass, with red glass stones.
~ 1908
Design: Albin Müller
H: 26.5 cm   W: 11.7 cm

Joseph Maria Olbrich

Born in Troppau in 1867, died in Düsseldorf in 1908. He was a pupil at the State Trade School in Vienna (1882-86) and studied at the Academy there (1890-93) under Baron von Hasenauer. As winner of the Academy's Prix de Rome, he went to study in Italy and North Africa (1893-94). He was a colleague of Otto Wagner (1894-99) and in 1897 a founder member of the Wiener Secession. He was invited to join the Artists' Colony in Darmstadt in 1899, where besides objects relating to all areas of the applied arts, he designed a number of buildings for the Artists' Colony Exhibitions in 1901, 1904 and 1908. He remained a member of the Artists' Colony until his death, but also carried out numerous external commissions (the Frauen-Rosenhof in Cologne, in 1905; the Warenhaus Tietz in Düsseldorf, in 1906-08, for example). Olbrich was a founder member of the Deutsche Werkbund in 1907.

269   *Candlestick*
Two-armed, polished pewter, with an abstract design; standing on a wide oval base. The shape of the candlestick is reminiscent of a female figure with raised arms.
1902
Monogram stamp:
Joseph Maria Olbrich and Edelzinn 1819 E. Hueck
H: 36.4 cm
Lit. Woeckel, *Jugendstil Sammlung,* Ill. No. 44a/b;
Kunsthandwerk um 1900 (Hessisches Landesmuseum, Darmstadt), p. 83, Ill. No. 85;
Europa 1900, Catalogue of the Ostend Exhibition, Ill. No. 86;
Art and Design at the Turn of the Century (The Museum of Modern Art, New York, 1959), Ill. p. 113.

270   *Floor-lamp*
From the music hall in the New Palace, Darmstadt 1902/03. Polished black maple, with various coloured inlays, brass and a blown-glass dome.
H: 168.5 cm

271 *Candlestick*
Two-branched on four feet. Silver and amethyst.
1901
Stamped with a crescent and eagle, and "800". Executed by P. Bruckman
H: 34.5 cm   W: 17.5 cm

272 *Candelabrum*
With two arms on a trellis-like stand. Brass, lacquered and polished wood, partly gilded, coloured glass and blue cabochons.
~ 1902
H: 168 cm

Orivit

Factory producing artistic metalware (joint-stock company), Cologne-Ehrenfeld. Formerly the Rheinish Ferd. Hub. Schmitz bronze foundry. After 1901 the firm used the registered trademark "Orivit" and "Schmitz Edelzinn". It took over the Württembergische Metallwarenfabrik in 1906.

273 *Table-lamp*
Silberzinn base. Two female figures with outstretched arms support the lampshades made of a green cased ice glass (Bohemian).
~ 1900
Marked: Orivit
H: 54 cm   Ø: 30 cm

274 Candelabrum
Five-branched. Standing on a
round base is a stylized figure of a
woman, whose arms swing out to
support the candle holders.
~ 1900
Marked: Orivit Köln-Braunsfeld
H: 42 cm   W: 31 cm

276 Table-lamp
An ornamental curving pewter
base flowing up into a stylized
flower, on which are hanging
strings of glass pearls.
~ 1900
Marked: Orivit
H: 35 cm   Ø: 19 cm

275 Candlestick
Pewter and crystal glass.
Hexagonal base.
~ 1905
Marked: OAG (Orivit) 3934
H: 28 cm

Osiris

Metalware factory producing small *objets d'art*.
Founded around 1900 as the Walter Scherf & Co.
pewter foundry, it was amalgamated in 1906 with
the firm of ISIS-Werke, Nuremberg. The
signature "Orion" is also used.

277 *Candelabrum*
Three-armed, pewter, gilded.
The base has six ornamental
knobs.
Design: Walter Scherf and
Hermann Gradl
Marked: Osiris 505
H: 25 cm

Bernhard Pankok

Born in Münster, Westphalia, in 1872, died in Munich in 1943. He was a painter (particularly of portraits), craftsman, architect, sculptor, and graphic artist. The son of a joiner, he studied at the Academies in Düsseldorf and Berlin. He was in Munich from 1892 to 1902 and was a founder member of the Vereinigte Werkstätten. After 1902 he was in Stuttgart, where he took over as principal of the Lehr- und Versuchsanstalten in 1903 and as director of the State School of Arts and Crafts from 1913. He conceived the entire catalogue for the German section at the World Exhibition in Paris in 1900. Pankok is known as one of the most outstanding exponents of the German Jugendstil.

278 *Candelabrum*
Twelve-branched. Brass.
~ 1901
Designed by Bernhard Pankok.
Manufactured by the Vereinigte Werkstätten für Kunst im Handwerk, Munich
H: 41 cm   W: 41.5 cm

Vereinigte Werkstätten

Founded in 1898 by F. A. O. Krüger, who directed the firm until 1912. The Vereinigte Werkstätten arose out of the collaboration of a number of leading figures in the German applied arts field after the Munich Glass Palace Exhibition of 1897 (Munich Secession). In 1902 H. Obrist and W. von Debschitz, together with the members of the Vereinigte Werkstätten, founded the Experimental Studios for the Applied and Fine Arts. The aims of the Vereinigte Werkstätten, like those of the Wiener Werkstätte, were to promote high quality craftsmanship in the applied arts by producing objects – primarily small *objets d'art*, furniture and household goods – from designs by leading artists. B. Pankok, R. Riemerschmid, Th. Schmutz-Baudiss and A. Niemeyer were all long-standing members of the Vereinigte Werkstätten.

279 *Hanging lamp*
Silvered brass. Hand-wrought.
~ 1905
Marked: 9531
H: 138 cm   Ø: 92 cm

Bruno Paul

Born in Seifhennersdorf in 1874, died in Berlin in 1968. From 1886 to 1894 he studied at the School of Arts and Crafts in Dresden, and after 1894 at the Academy in Munich. He was a founder member of the Vereinigte Werkstätten in Munich in 1898. From 1907 until 1933, he held a teaching post at the Museum of Applied Arts in Berlin.

280 *Hanging lamp*
Twelve candles on matt-glass saucers are arranged in a circle and joined together by looping chains of crystal-glass balls, decorated with regularly spaced teardrops, also made of crystal glass. The interior part is arranged like a fountain of water constructed of glass drops. The lamp frame is silvered brass.
1926
H: 100 cm   Ø: 120 cm

281 *Candlestick*
Bronze.
Designed by Bruno Paul for the Vereinigte Werkstätten.
H: 25 cm

Richard Riemerschmid

Born and died in Munich (1868-1957). An architect and versatile designer in the field of the applied arts. He was a pupil at the Munich Art Academy from 1888 until 1890 and a founder member of the Vereinigte Werkstätten für Kunst im Handwerk in Munich in 1898. He designed the interiors of the Munich Playhouse in 1901 and directed the Munich School of Arts and Crafts from 1912 to 1924. He directed the Cologne Trade Schools from 1926. Riemerschmid was the leading artist of the Munich Jugendstil with its very pronounced individual stamp.

282   *Table-lamp*
1899
Design: Richard Riemerschmid, Munich
H: 38.5 cm
Lit. *Bayern* Catalogue (1972), No. 2100

283   *Hanging lamp*
Brass canopy. Crystal balls and conical-shaped glass prisms are suspended on fine chains.
1901
H: 63 cm
Ill. *Die Kunst*, VI (1902)

284 *Pair of candlesticks*
Stylized branches in polished
bronze on a round base.
1898
Manufacture: Vereinigte
Werkstätten für Kunst im
Handwerk, Munich
H: 36 cm
Ill. *Dekorative Kunst*, II (1898),
p. 152

285 *Table-lamp*
Brass, with three lights.
~ 1906
Designed by Richard
Riemerschmid for the Dresdner
Werkstätten für Handwerk
H: 35.5 cm

286 *Ceiling-lamp*
Gilded brass with three small
green glass shades that have a
slight lustre.
~ 1912
Design: Richard Riemerschmid
H: 50 cm   Ø: 87 cm
Lit. *Die Kunst*, IV (1901)

Franz von Stuck

Born in Tettenweis (lower Bavaria) in 1863, died in Munich in 1928. Painter, illustrator and sculptor in bronze, he was knighted in 1906. He was a founder member of the Secession and a professor at the Munich Academy. Influenced by A. Böcklin, he painted principally allegorical subjects depicting nudes and mythological beings. Stuck was the most important Jugendstil painter in Munich. The Stuck-Villa, built to his plans, was a Jugendstil attempt to create a *Gesamtkunstwerk* (a total work of art).

287 *Hanging lamp*
Bronze frame suspended on cords, with six small glass shades (Johann Loetz Wtw.) coloured an iridescent yellowish orange. The lamp hangs in the Stuck-Villa in Munich. It was not possible to measure the lamp because of the great height of the ceiling.

Heinrich Vogeler

Born in Bremen in 1872, died in Kasachstan, Russia, in 1942. Painter, graphic artist, designer of *objets d'art*, etc., interior designer and architect. The son of a Bremen businessman, he studied painting at the Art Academy in Düsseldorf (1890-93). In 1894 he settled in Worpswede, where he bought and redesigned the Barkenhof in 1895. He set up his own printing press there and in the following four years produced thirty-two etchings. In 1898 he travelled to Italy where he became friendly with the poet Rainer Maria Rilke. For part of 1898 he was in Munich working for the Insel publishing house. In 1901 he married Martha Schröder. In the following years he produced numerous etchings. From 1903 to 1905 he worked on the Guldenkammer in Bremen town hall. He and his brother Franz set up a furniture workshop in 1908. Between 1900 and 1910, apart from his work as a painter and graphic artist, Vogeler was also involved in designing jewellery, tableware, lamps, candelabra and other household items. He produced his last etchings in the years 1922-23. In 1923/24 he travelled to Russia for the first time and in 1931 finally emigrated there.

288 *Wall-bracket*
Polished iron, with two
candleholders; abstract design.
1902
Manufactured by:
M. Seifert, Dresden
H: 31 cm   W: 24 cm
Lit *Deutsche Kunst und
Dekoration* (April 1902), p. 325

Emil Rudolf Weiss

Born in Lahr, Baden, in 1875, died in Meersburg in 1942. Painter and graphic illustrator, and designer in the applied arts. He studied at the Academies in Karlsruhe and Stuttgart and also at the Académie Julian in Paris. Weiss was a working member of "Pan" from 1895/96.
A year later he took up his extraordinarily successful engagement as book illustrator for the publishers Eugen Diederichs, S. Fischer and Insel.
Karl Ernst Osthaus obtained work for him in the Folkwang Museum in Essen from 1903 to 1906. From 1907 to 1933 Emil Rudolf Weiss worked in the educational department of the Museum of Applied Arts and in the Combined State Schools for Fine and Applied Arts, both in Berlin. He was married to the sculptress Renée Sintenis.

289   *Table-lamp*
Light-brown cased glass. An etched landscape with water. Shade and base both illuminated. ~ 1898
Sign. E. R. Weiss
H: 45 cm   Ø: 14 cm

Theodor Wende

Born in Berlin in 1883, died in Pforzheim in 1968. He studied at the Drawing Academy in Hanau and at the School of Arts and Crafts in Berlin under J. Wackerle and Bruno Paul. He worked in Berlin until 1913 and was then asked to join the Artists' Colony in Darmstadt. In 1914, at the third exhibition at the Artists' Colony, he showed jewellery and works in metal. He was appointed professor at the School of Arts and Crafts, now the Master School for German Precious Metals and the Jewellery Trade, in Pforzheim in 1921.

290   *Candlestick*
Shaft painted with Indian ink and opaque colours. Candlestick of silver.
Marked with a symbol of four candles and "Berlin 1911 Th. Wende"
H: 52 cm   W: 34.1 cm

Wilkens & Söhne

Silverware factory, Bremen. The firm was founded in 1810 by M. H. Wilkens (1782-1869), who had just become a master. The factory was continued by his sons Dietrich (-1876), Philipp (1813-74) and Wilhelm (-1895). The firm was represented at the World Exhibition in Turin in 1902. Heinrich Vogeler was one of the designers who worked for Wilkens. The firm still exists today as "Wilkens Bremer Silberwaren AG".

291 *Pair of candlesticks*
Day and Night. Silver.
~ 1901
Marked: "M. H. Wilkens & Söhne, Bremen"
H: 33 cm   W: 32.5 cm

292 *Candlestick*
Three-branched. Silver.
~ 1930
Marked: "Wilkens & Söhne, Bremen"
H: 60 cm   W: 30 cm

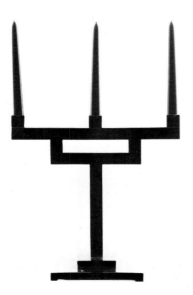

Württembergische Metallwarenfabrik (WMF)

Founded in 1853 by Daniel Straub in Geislingen under the name "Metallwarenfabrik Straub & Schweizer", later "Straub & Sohn". It was amalgamated with the "Metallwarenfabrik A. Ritter & Co.", Esslingen, and became a joint-stock company under the name "Württembergische Metallwarenfabrik". In 1900 it was a large concern with three thousand employees, producing silver-plated and nickelled tableware and decorative pieces, cutlery, copper and brass articles, galvanized bronzes and glass products which were made in the attached glassworks founded in 1883.

Apart from the head office, there were factories in Göppingen, Vienna, Berlin, Cologne and Warsaw and distribution branches in the large German cities.

From its early allegiance to Renaissance, Neo-Rococo and Sheffield ware, the firm switched entirely to the Jugendstil after 1900. During 1914-18 it produced only war-related materials and all branches were closed due to economic pressure. After the end of the war the firm began to expand and today employs seven thousand people in Germany and abroad.

293　*Candelabrum*
Four-branched. The shaft is in the shape of a girl; her flowing dress forms the base. Cast and silvered brass.
~ 1900

Marked: WMF and B
(= Britannia alloy)
H: 48 cm

294　*Pair of candlesticks*
Silver-plated brass.
~ 1903
Marked: WMF
H: 28 cm

295 *Pair of candlesticks*
Single holder, polished pewter
and brass. A female figure with
outstretched arm; her dress
swings up from the circular foot.
1903
WMF
Marked: B ... (illegible)
..OX 269, 269 A
H: 24 cm
Two-armed candlestick in the
background.
Stamped: 3
(H: 35 cm)

297 *Pair of candlesticks*
Silver-plated brass
~ 1900
Marked: WMF I/o OX
H: 22.5 cm

296 *Pair of candlesticks*
Britannia Metal.
~ 1905
Marked: WMF B
H: 15 cm   W: 7 cm

No closer identification

298   Ceiling-light
Opal-coloured nautilus-shell
pieces set in lead form the bowl
which is encircled by a ring of
orange cabochons. Copperplate
frame.
~ 1900
Designed by Montelius (?)
⌀: 30 cm

299   Hanging lamp
Brass rods, interrupted by small
illuminated spheres made of
yellow, white and blue glass
stones. The bowl is ornamented
with the same leaded glass
stones.
~ 1900
Design: Montelius
H: 90 cm   ⌀: 35 cm

300   Hanging lamp
Beaten brass. Cone-shaped
centre piece and tube-shaped
side pieces made of colourless
moulded glass.
~ 1928
H: 154 cm

301 *Hanging lamp*
Brass. The rods form an abstract design. A light bulb has been fitted into the central shaft and four milk-glass tubes serve as light fittings.
~ 1927
Designed by Krüger, Berlin
Similar models are depicted in *Kunst und Dekoration*
H: 126 cm

304 *Table-lamp*
Chromium-plated metal. The triple-vaulted shade is interrupted with moulded-glass balls.
~ 1928
H: 69 cm   Ø: 45 cm

302 *Hanging lamp*
Six lights. Chromium-plated metal with sheets of clear glass; the illuminated bowl is milk glass. Spherical body.
~ 1926
Designed by Krüger, Berlin
H: 150 cm   Ø: 41 cm

305 *Pair of standard lamps*
Brass with white milk-glass panels. Identical except for the construction of the shades. (The left one pagoda-shaped, the right one smoothly tapered.)
~ 1930
H: 164 cm   Ø: 50 cm

303 *Candelabrum*
Five-branched. Brass. Geometrical construction.
~ 1926
Bauhaus (?)
H: 43 cm   W: 41 cm

307   Table-lamp
Foot, shaft and dome are of brass.
The hammered shade is
decorated with inserted coloured
glass stones.
~ 1910
Montelius (?)
H: 51 cm   ∅: 25.5 cm

306   Writing-desk lamp
Eloxated aluminium. Mushroom-
shaped, with a Constructivist
design.
~ 1928
H: 65 cm   ∅: 40 cm

308 *Table-lamp*
Chromium, with a white glass
sphere and a female nude.
1930
H: 49 cm

309 *Writing-desk lamp*
Hammered copperplate, with
glass rods. Mushroom-shaped, on
an eight-cornered foot. Has a
dimmer.
~ 1920
H: 65 cm
⌀: 45 cm

310 *Candlestick*
Two-armed, gilded pewter, with
a design of hemlock flowers.
~ 1900
Sign. R. Pirlon
H: 25 cm   W: 27 cm

312 *Pair of candlesticks*
Thickly plated pewter with a rose
design. The tapered top has three
handles.
~ 1910
Sign. (illegible)
H: 26 cm

311 *Candlestick*
Three-branched. Brass. Abstract
design.
~ 1910
H: 43.5 cm

V GREAT BRITAIN

Doulton

Royal potteries, manufacturing ceramic and porcelain at Lambeth in London, and at Burslem in Staffordshire.

Founded by John Doulton in 1815, in Vauxhall. His later partner was John Watts. The firm styled itself "Doulton & Watts". In 1826 it was transferred to Lambeth. Sir Henry Doulton (1820-97) took over the firm in 1835. In 1858 John Watts died and the firm was renamed "Henry Doulton & Co."

The following years saw the patenting of various new methods in the production of porcelain and stoneware. A branch was opened in Burslem, near Stoke-on-Trent, in 1882. The firm began to wane in importance in 1899. The factory in Lambeth was closed down in 1956. The branch in Burslem exists today under the name "Doulton Fine China Ltd, Royal Doulton Potteries, Burslem". In the second half of the nineteenth century, production included earthenware, faïence, porcelain and terracotta for wall coverings.

314 *Pair of candlesticks*
Faïence. A blue and brown ornamental design.
~ 1900
Sign. Royal Doulton
H: 18 cm

313 *Pair of candlesticks*
Stoneware in pale blue, dark blue and yellow.
Stamped: Royal Doulton 672 5625
RB yu
2nd candlestick: stamped 5626
RB S 80

Christopher Dresser

(1834-1904). He was a botanist, designer and writer, who was already designing silver objects in 1860. He worked in simple, austere lines, allowing the natural beauty of his material its full expression. Cubic forms are already evident in his work before the turn of the century. He often used the galvanic method of silverplating, and also worked in copper, glass and clay.

315 *Candlestick*
On a small dish, serving as a smoker's accessory. Silver and ebony.
Birmingham 1894/95
Sign. Christopher Dresser
H: 12 cm

Liberty & Co.   Archibald Knox

Metalware firm in London. Founded in 1875 by Arthur Lasenby Liberty (1843-1917). The firm sold the products of a series of jewellery and silverware manufacturers, who were commissioned by them, and played an important part in spreading the Modern Style (Art Nouveau) in England and on the Continent. The Stile Liberty became the term for the Jugendstil in Italy. After 1901 the firm of W. H. Haseler worked exclusively for Liberty. Archibald Knox

and Arthur Gaskin were amongst the most important designers. The firm's pewter production ran under the name "Cymric" after 1899, and "Tudric" after 1902.
Archibald Knox was born in 1864 and died in 1933. He was a designer of silver and pewter ware and a silversmith. Knox supplied the English firm of Liberty & Co. with over four hundred designs and also made silver items for them.

316 *Candlestick*
Pewter, with an abstract floral design.
~ 1903
Marked: Liberty & Co., tudric 023
H: 14 cm

317 *Candlestick*
Pewter. Geometrical design.
~ 1903
Marked: Liberty & Co., tudric 022
H: 13.5 cm

318 *Candlestick*
Polished pewter, with two
holders.
1905
Design: Archibald Knox
Marked: Liberty & Co.
H: 28.5 cm

319 *Candlestick*
Pewter. Abstract design.
~ 1904
Designed by Archibald Knox (?)
Marked: Liberty & Co.
H: 3.5 cm   W: 18.5 cm

320 *Pair of candlesticks*
Pewter, so-called "Britannia
Metal".
1903
Designed by Archibald Knox
Probably made by Haseler,
Birmingham
Marked: English Pewter 0223
Made in England
H: 23 cm

321 *Candlestick*
Candle holder in polished
pewter, with an abstract design.
~ 1902
Stamped: Cymric 0218-5
Design: Archibald Knox (?)
H: 18.5 cm

Ashly-Smith Neate

Dates not known.

322 *Wall-bracket*
Two-armed candlestick. Beaten-
copper body, with an abstract
design and three pale-blue glass
cabochons. The whole is
mounted on an oakwood base. On
the back is an old exhibition label.
1902
Designed and made by Ashly-
Smith Neate
H: 58.5 cm   W: 24.5 cm

Compare *The Studio*,
XXIV (1902), p. 177, Plate
"International Studio
Exhibition". The candlestick
illustrated there is falsely
described (printing mistake) as
made by S. Asby-Sheare. A hand-
written label on the back of our
example shows without doubt
that the above-mentioned artist
made it.

323 *Pair of candlesticks*
Silver gilt with a hammered shaft.
Silver mark (London 1902)
Sign. Stewart Devlin
H: 25 cm   Ø: 7 cm (Foot)

VI NETHERLANDS

Jan Eisenloeffel

Born in Amsterdam in 1876, died in Laren in 1957. Dutch silversmith and craftsman. From 1892 he attended the National School of Drawing in Amsterdam, and occasionally did practical work in W. Hoeker's silverware workshops. He worked for them after 1896, and was director of the metal section of Amstelhoek. In 1900 he stayed temporarily in St Petersburg, where he visited Peter Fabergé, and Moscow. During 1908 he collaborated with the Vereinigte Werkstätten für Kunst im Handwerk in Munich.

In 1909 he settled in Laren near Amsterdam. He was awarded a gold medal at the Applied Arts Exhibitions in Turin (1902), Arnheim, Dresden (1904) and Munich (1908).

The stereometric forms of his work – which is almost wholly without ornament – accentuate the structure of the metal. Eisenloeffel was one of the great innovators of metalwork in the applied arts, and the extraordinary severity of his style appears far in advance of his times.

324　*Small oil lamp*
Brass. Egg-shaped reservoir with a lid. A small snuffer hangs on a chain.
~ 1900
Marked with a running ostrich
H: 21.5 cm

Kölln & Hornig

325　*Pair of candlesticks*
Two-armed. Brass with dull finish and insertions of vertical rectangular cut crystal.
~ 1926
Designed by Walter Gropius
Made by Kölln & Hornig, Den Haag
H: 31.7 cm　W: 25 cm

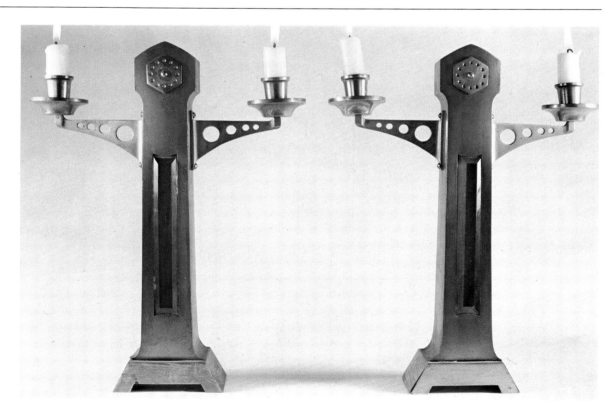

Urania

Metalware factory manufacturing *objets d'art*, and pewter foundry at Maastricht. From about 1900 until 1910 they produced tableware of all kinds, including those pieces signed "Juventa".

326 *Candlestick*
Three-armed.
~ 1903
Marked: Juventa Primametal
H: 40.5 cm

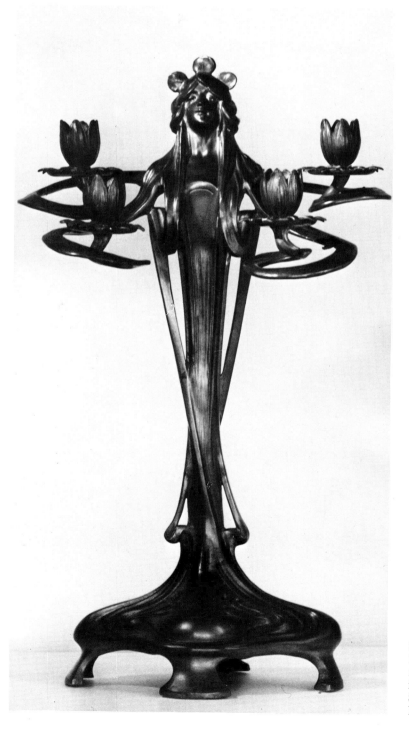

327 *Candelabrum*
Four-branched, pewter, representing a stylized female figure on a round base.
Sign. Imperial-Zinn No. 4786
H: 47 cm   W: 28 cm

328 *Pair of candlesticks*
Brass with a pewter coating.
~ 1902
Marked: Juventa
H: 29 cm

329 *Candelabrum*
Four-branched; polished pewter,
with an abstract design; on a
round foot.
1900
Marked: Urania 1209
H: 34.5 cm

330 *Pair of candlesticks*
Silvered pewter.
~ 1904
Marked: Juventa
H: 19 cm   W: 11 cm

VII USA

The US Art Bent Glass Company

Founded in Hardford, Connecticut. The exact date is not known, but the company must already have been in existence around 1900 as a catalogue for the year 1910 features various hanging lamps made of bent glass (glass blown from a single piece and used in the manufacture of lampshades), which was a speciality of theirs. The same catalogue also includes other types of art glass, such as opaline, which was used in mosaic-patterned shades for table- and hanging lamps.

The diameter of the largest lamps was as much as 70 cm. Only recently have experts shown an interest in the superbly crafted creations of this highly versatile firm.

331 *Hanging lamp*
Ruby-red, honey-yellow and green opaline, decorated with a garland of flowers. In the middle of the blooms are jewelled-glass cabochons.
~ 1908
⌀: 57.5 cm
Compare Revi, *American Art Nouveau Glass*, p. 303, Ill. No. 1058

332 *Hanging lamp*
Honey-coloured opaline with yellow streaks. Hanging strings of pearls in a rose design.
1910
⌀: 60 cm

333 *Hanging lamp*
Opaline in a honey colour with streaks of brown and violet. Rhombus insets of yellow glass, and round, coloured jewel-glass drops.
~ 1908
∅: 58 cm

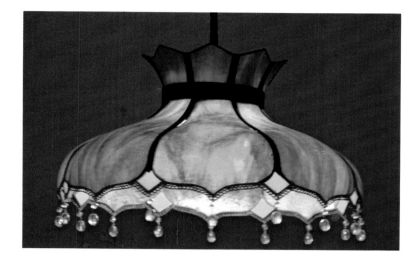

334 *Hanging lamp*
Pale-blue opaline with hanging strings of pearls in black, pink, blue and yellow.
~ 1910
∅: 60 cm

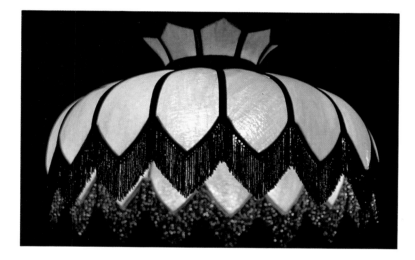

335 *Hanging lamp*
Green opaline. Bronze frame decorated with abstract ornaments and beading of pearl and glass rods, in the shape of a rose.
~ 1909
∅: 55 cm

Bradley & Hubbard Manufacturing Company

The location of this firm is not known. Bradley & Hubbard made petroleum lamps and chandeliers around 1840. All pieces were signed with their name. In about 1900, after Tiffany had shown his lamps with such great success at various world exhibitions, Bradley & Hubbard began to produce electric lamps with shades of coloured mosaic glass and with iridescent glass blown directly into the metal frame (bronze, brass, etc.).

336 *Table-lamp*
Greenish yellow and red opaline with an ornamental brass frame. Base of polished bronze.
Date: 20.10.1908
Sign. (both shade and foot) Bradley & Hubbard
H: 53 cm ∅: 37 cm

337 *Table-lamp*
Yellowish marbled opaline with a bronze mount. The shade is decorated with a ring of poppy flowers and a bronze relief of poppy flowers also adorns the base.
~ 1905
Sign. (in a triangle) Bradley & Hubbard; in the middle of the triangle an oil lamp as signature
H: 50 cm ∅: 41 cm

338 *Table-lamp*
Blue and olive-green opaline, with yellow stripes. Decorative bronze elements on base and frame of shade.
~ 1900
H: 48 cm ∅: 40 cm

339 *Ceiling-light*
Opaline. Green leaves arranged in a star shape with yellow and ruby-red geometrical ornamentation. Bronze rods.
~ 1900
∅: 60 cm

340 *Hanging lamp*
Sunrise Lamp. Multicoloured opaline, depicting the sun (at the crown), with its rays pouring down on a variety of plant life, including water lilies. The leading on this unusually large lamp is finished with silver-foil.
~ 1900
∅: 60 cm

Crest & Co.

341 Hanging lamp
Trumpet-shaped. The top part is
leaded opaline with a crown of
polished bronze and two circles
of ruby-red glass. The lower
section is in milky opaline with an
irregular edge and a design of
roses and green leaves.
~ 1906
∅: 52 cm

342 Table-lamp
Honey-yellow opaline with a
design of orange flowers and
green leaves. Telescope-shaped
base of polished and decorated
bronze.
~ 1905
Sign. Crest Co., Chicago
(between the frames)
H: 67 cm   ∅: 45.5 cm
See also Documentation.

343 *Table-lamp*
Leaded opaline in yellow, green and red, with a design of tulip leaves and flowers and a wavy edge. Finial of lattice-like pierced bronze. The bronze base is in the form of a stylized tree with roots.
~ 1905
H: 54 cm   Ø: 42 cm

344 *Table-lamp*
Leaded opaline in green, blue, pink and white, with a small crown of jewel glass. Ornamental bronze foot.
~ 1910
H: 45 cm   Ø: 35 cm

345 *Table-lamp*
Yellow and ruby-red opaline, with a stylized flower design. Ornamental bronze foot.
~ 1910
H: 50 cm   Ø: 40 cm

A. Douglas Nash Corporation

Douglas Nash (birth-date unknown; died in New York in 1940) worked for a long time for Louis C. Tiffany as designer and glass-blower. In 1928 he bought the Corona Glassworks which Tiffany had owned. His amicable relationship with the Tiffany Studios meant that Nash was able to display his glass objects in Tiffany's shops. They were principally made from chintz glass and bubbly glass, two types which Nash had developed in the course of experiments while still with Tiffany. Tiffany was not especially impressed by these coloured glasses which were also enormously difficult to produce, and so gave Nash the production rights. Nash's glass was particularly beautiful. He showed his creations for the first time in his own personal exhibition at the Waldorf Astoria Hotel in New York. Nash only invited artists to the opening, leaving out the entire trade. He was spoken of in New York as "crazy Nash". He was plagued by bad luck in his business ventures. Hardly had he brought out his very beautiful and colourful chintz and bubbly glass, when the Czechoslovakian glass industry undercut him by producing an enormous number of cheap copies, and Nash had to close his own production on financial grounds.

There are only a few candlesticks and glass lamp bases known to have been designed by him. His earliest pieces are signed with the letters A. D. N. A.; after 1928, his work is signed "Nash". See Documentation.

Fostoria Glass Specialty Company

This firm was founded in 1899 by J. D. Crouse, his son J. Robert Crouse, Henry A. Tremaine and B. G. Tremaine in Fostoria, Ohio. It produced its first art glass around 1901 and soon specialized in lustre-decorated coloured glass, to which the trademark "IRIS" was given in 1912. Table-lamps with illuminated bases in blown glass similar to those produced by the Nancy school, artistically constructed shades for oil lamps and numerous small lampshades, equalling in quality those of Steuben or Loetz, accounted for ninety percent of the Fostoria production. Fostoria was taken over by the General Electric Company of New York, who had bought up all the patents, and in 1917 General Electric closed down the firm. See Documentation.

Handel Company Inc.

Philip Handel (1866-1914), the founder of this firm, came from an immigrant German family. His parents were farmers who encouraged his liking for the applied arts. At the age of fourteen, he became an apprentice at the Meriden Flint-Glass Company, where he quickly showed a special talent for working in decorative glass. With Adolph Eyden, in 1885, he founded the studio Eyden and Handel Glass Decorators in Meriden. Handel bought his partner out in 1893 and changed the workshop name to "Handel & Co." and in 1904 altered it once again to "The Handel Company Inc." and took in four partners. Philip Handel died on 14 July 1914 at the age of forty-eight. His widow, Fanny Handel, directed the workshop until 1918 and transferred it in 1919 to Handel's cousin, William F. Handel, who directed it until 14 March 1934. The workshop closed down permanently in 1936.

Philip Handel's main area of glass production was the design and manufacture of table- and hanging lamps, and his speciality were hand-painted glass lamps. He was granted a patent in the USA in 1904 and in England in 1905 for his "chipping glass", which was produced by sandblasting the still warm coloured glass to produce an ice-like surface. As Handel used this glass in almost all his mosaic shades, his lamps are easily distinguishable from those of Tiffany. It is curious that twenty-odd years earlier, in 1883, exactly the same method was patented in Germany. Handel developed many new methods for manufacturing decorative glass and was, after Tiffany, the most important American manufacturer in the field. Also typical of Handel's creations is the use of glass stones with an almost metallic effect, so-called "jewelled glass" which only lights up when the source of light is turned on. In 1924 the firm ceased manufacturing the lamps which are so valued as collector's pieces today.

Handel's preferred motifs include wild roses, irises, poppies and branches filled with birds. Other designers working alongside Handel include: Henry Bedigie, Mrs F. Hirschfeld, the Dutchman Gubisch and a man named Rochette, presumably a Frenchman.

A minor scandal arose around 1902 when it was discovered that Henry O. Schmidt, a German emigrant who worked for Handel, was also working for the Tiffany Studios on the side, and had, moreover, set up his own small workshop, where he produced lamps strongly resembling those of Handel and Tiffany. For this reason, it is not always possible to know whether the lamps designed by Schmidt, mostly unsigned, should in fact be attributed to either Tiffany or Handel. The contention that Philip Handel himself worked for Tiffany is incorrect.

347 *Table-lamp*
Dogwood. Favrile glass; the mosaic parts soldered with copper (instead of lead). Colours: white, yellow, red, green. The bronze base, representing a stylized tree, has a dark brown patina.
~ 1902
Sign. (Shade) HANDEL
Sign. (Base) HANDEL, and marked: 33
H: 60.5 cm   Ø: 45.5 cm

346 *Hanging lamp*
Tulip flower in opaline set in copper. The petals are red, streaked with a delicate blue and white; the calyx is dark greenish blue. The pedicel, which forms a hook, is in bronze.
~ 1900
H: 58.5 cm   Ø: 34 cm

348 *Hanging lamp*
Red, green and yellow opaline, speckled with carnelian. Design of roses and an irregular border.
1901
∅: 53 cm

349 *Hanging lamp*
The shade, in coloured opaline with leaded mosaic, narrows to a cone. Colours: blue, violet, green, various reds and golden yellow. Design: peonies, with stems made of chipping glass.
1904
∅: 68 cm

350 *Hanging lamp*
Opaline, shaded in many colours and set with cherries made of jewelled glass. Design of birds on cherry twigs and an irregular, scalloped border.
1903
∅: 60 cm

351 *Table lamp*
Meander-patterned opaline in blue and emerald green, with a border of moonstone-coloured jewelled glass top and bottom. The bronze base has a floral design.
1899
Sign. (on the base): Handel Company, Meriden, Connecticut
H: 57.5 cm   Ø: 41 cm

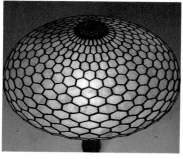

352 *Table-lamp*
Yellowish green opaline leaded in a honeycomb design. Pierced bronze finial and bronze foot.
1910
H: 58 cm   Ø: 54 cm

353 *Table lamp*
Opaline: yellow ground with white and pink honeysuckle flowers and green leaves. The lamp has a particularly beautiful bronze base with a lily-pad design and a swan-neck fitting.
~ 1900
Sign. (on the top of the shade)
Handel Lamps; (on the base)
Handel and Pat'd No. 97664
H: 65 cm   ∅: 50 cm

354 *Table-lamp*
Yellowish green opaline with honey-coloured streaks. The leading in the crown is arranged into an abstract design. Finial and foot are bronze.
~ 1905
H: 58 cm   ∅: 47 cm

355 *Table-lamp*
Honey-yellow opaline decorated
with a wreath of pale-blue iris
flowers and green leaves.
Mounted on a contemporary
bronze base.
~ 1905
H: 71 cm   Ø: 50 cm

356 *Table-lamp*
Green opaline with yellow
flowers. Scalloped border
which curves inwards.
Bronze base and finial
~ 1905
H: 62 cm   Ø: 40 cm

357 *Table-lamp*
Pink, emerald and pale-green
opaline, mounted on a bronze
base. Design: apple-blossom
wreath with leaves.
1904
H: 60.5 cm   ∅: 42 cm

358 *Table-lamp*
Brown, yellow, green and white
leaded opaline. Design: flowering
narcissus. Crown and lower
border in chipping glass. On a
bronze foot.
~ 1904
Sign. HANDEL
H: 67 cm   ∅: 48 cm

359 *Table-lamp*
Opaline, decorated with blue
flowers, green leaves and twigs.
The flower pistils are jewelled
glass. Bronze base.
1900
H: 51 cm   Ø: 39.5 cm
(There is an identical model with
pink flowers by L. C. Tiffany.)

360 *Table-lamp*
Top part: yellow opaline in a
bronze frame. Undulating border
with a landscape of bronze trees
on a reddish opaline ground.
Bronze base.
~ 1904
Sign. HANDEL (Shade and base)
H: 59 cm   Ø: 47 cm

361 *Table-lamp*
Opaline in honey yellow, pink, red, pale green, emerald and carnelian. The crown is set with diamond-shaped jewelled-glass cabochons. Design: roses with twigs and leaves, running into a serrated border. Bronze base with a greenish-black patina, modelled on a tree-trunk with roots.
1900
H: 77 cm   ∅: 60 cm

362 *Table-lamp*
Two-armed. The shade has a convex edge. Moss-coloured glass with an etched abstract design.
~ 1902
H: 52 cm   W: 59 cm
H (Shade): 12 cm
∅ (Shade): 18 cm
Both shades signed inside:
MOSSERINE "HANDEL" 6998
Under the base is a fabric label:
Handel-Lamps

363 *Table-lamp*
Red, pink, pale-green and
emerald opaline, with a design of
phlox flowers. Mounted on a
contemporary bronze base.
~ 1905
H: 60 cm   ∅: 46.5 cm

364 *Table-lamp*

Rose Tree. The shade, open at the top, is composed of branches (bronze, with a green patina) which terminate in rose blooms and leaves in red and green opaline. The particularly beautiful foot (bronze, with a green patina) represents the stylized stem of a tall rose tree. This extremely rare model marks a high point in the production of the Handel Company Inc., Meriden, Connecticut.
1901
Design: Philip Handel
H: 66 cm   Ø 51 cm

365 *Hanging lamp*
Opaline, decorated with pink
chrysanthemums between dark-
green leaves on a yellow ground.
Irregular border.
~ 1905
∅: 57 cm

The Lustre Art Glass Company

Martin Bach's son-in-law, Conrad Vahlsing, founded the Lustre Art Glass Company on Long Island in 1920. (Martin Bach was the founder of the Quezal Glass firm.) The company only existed until 1923. Vahlsing had worked for years with his father-in-law and, like the latter, imitated Tiffany techniques. Apart from blown-glass lampshades, the firm is not known to have manufactured art glass.

Edward Miller & Company

The firm of Edward Miller was just one of a number of glassmaking concerns that grew up around Meriden, Connecticut, during the second half of the nineteenth century. Originally the firm produced decorative metal objects for use in home furnishings, including bases in bronze and other metals for oil lamps. In the patent office in Washington various trademarks are entered for Miller's oil-lamp bases. With the increased usage of electric light, Miller began constructing table-lamps and ceiling-lights. The opaline and mosaic glass used in his shades was supplied by the other local glassworks in Meriden.

367   *Table-lamp*
White, yellow and green opaline. An abstract design runs around an undulating border. On an ornamental bronze base.

~ 1908
Sign. E. M. & Co.
H: 55 cm   Ø: 35 cm

368   *Table-lamp*
Green and white opaline with a wreath of stylized leaves. The finial and quadrangular foot are bronze.
~ 1902
H: 60 cm   Ø: 40 cm

369   *Table-lamp*
Yellow, red and green opaline. Design: a garland of poppy flowers with applied bronze stamens. Cast-zinc base with an abstract design and greenish patina.
~ 1907
Sign. E. M. & Co.
H: 63 cm   Ø: 50 cm

366   *Table-lamp*
Opaline in green, yellow and carnelian on a bronze foot. Design: stylized autumn leaves.
1910
Sign. E. M. & Co.
H: 60 cm   Ø: 40 cm

Moran & Hastings Manufacturing Company

The year when the firm was founded is not known. A large catalogue for 1912 shows opaline lampshades with the most varied mosaic designs, both geometric and floral; also curved lampshades made of blown opaline, table-lamps of cut glass and lustre-glass shades. The latter may have been supplied by manufacturers such as Quezal or Steuben.

370 *Hanging lamp*
Trumpet-shaped, bent opaline in yellow, green, blue, brown, red and orange. The wide border has a design of bulrushes and a red water lily.
~ 1904
∅: 58 cm

371 *Table-lamp*
White, green, carnelian and honey-yellow opaline. Design: water lilies and bulrushes. Mounted on a contemporary bronze foot.
~ 1912
H: 59 cm   ∅: 46 cm

372 *Table-lamp*
The shade has large areas of coloured lustre glass held by a geometrical bronze frame. On a bronze base.
~ 1904
H: 52 cm   Ø: 48 cm

Pairpoint Manufacturing Company

Between 1880 and 1900 Pairpoint produced only metal lamp bases and holders. With the take-over of the Mt Washington Glass Company in 1900, the firm began manufacturing glass on an enormous scale: 350 glass-cutters and over a hundred glass-blowers were employed. The series produced by Pairpoint, however, were only a response to average tastes of the time and remained without particular artistic value. There is one significant exception to this: a new type of art glass called "tulip glass", which was designed by Albert Steffin and patented for Pairpoint in 1908.

373 *Table-lamp*
Green, yellow, red and blue opaline, with stylized tulip flowers and leaves. Burnished-brass base with a leaf design.
Sign. Pairpoint Corporation
H: 56 cm   Ø: 35 cm

374 *Table-lamp*
Yellow, brown, green and red opaline. A wavy plant design in tulip glass runs around the edge of the shade. Bronze finial and foot.
1908
Sign. Pairpoint Corporation
H: 60 cm   Ø: 45 cm

Quezal Art Glass & Decorating Company

The firm, named after the colourful South American bird, was founded in 1901 in New York, and continued operating until 1924.

Its founder was Martin Bach who had worked for Tiffany as a glass technician and, to Tiffany's great annoyance, copied his particular techniques in making lustre colours in his own business. Bach, who was not himself an artist, invited Thomas Johnson to join him; following Johnson, Percy Britton and William Wiedebine then became partners in the firm. Tiffany altered the colours of his lustre glass and the new technique remained such a closely guarded secret that it died with him. Besides vases and other art-glass objects, Quezal produced, in particular, blown lustre-glass lampshades. The glass often bears the etched design of the Quezal bird's feather. Quezal shades are highly valued by collectors in the USA. The typical iridescent colours of Quezal designs are: red, green, blue, platinum, gold (similar to Tiffany's Favrile glass, but almost always decorated with whitish opaline), with decorative additions of yellow, deep brown and opal.

Steuben Glassworks

This important glass firm was founded on 11 March 1907 in New York. It still exists today and its name is associated with designers and artists of genius such as John Sporer (paper-weights), Bolas Manikowsky (cut and etched cased glass), Arthur Janssen (Aurene glass) and the Englishman Frederick Carder (1863-1963), who was, after Tiffany, the most important technician and designer of American glass. Throughout his long life, Carder worked incessantly on new artistic designs and manufacturing techniques. He directed Steuben for sixty years and it is to him that the firm owes its position of international importance.

At the beginning of this century Steuben made almost every known kind of art glass: Gold and Blue Aurene, a type of Favrile glass with and without decoration, *pâte-de-verre*, *Verre de Soie*, Jade glass, a stained opaline in Rosaline, Alabaster, blue jade, green jade and amethyst jade shades, transparent, coloured art glass, crystal with cut or applied decoration, Ruby glass, Cluthra and Cintra glass, cased glass, etched or cut, glass with coloured inclusions, Florentia glass with its icy quality, opalescent glass, Calcite and ivory glass, inlaid art glass, *millefiori* – similar to Murano glass, *Matsu-no-ke* – a clear crystal glass after a Japanese model, sparingly decorated in blue or pink (the production of this glass had to be stopped for reasons of patent, which is why there are no signed pieces of *Matsu-no-ke* glass), paper-weights and, finally, pressed glass and sculptured glass similar to those produced by Lalique. The list of Steuben models is almost too long to enumerate. Such an important glassware firm was naturally also involved with lighting and over the years produced numerous lamps and chandeliers in its own personal style.

375 *Hanging lamp*
Polished bronze. From a large
ceiling plate hang four shades of
Favrile glass with bronze mounts.
1905
Sign. Steuben
H: 54 cm   Ø: 52 cm

376 *Small table-lamp*
The bronze base represents a
water-lily leaf with a bud and
supports a Favrile-glass shade,
decorated with a wavy pattern.
~ 1903
Sign. (Base) Handel
Sign. (Glass) Steuben
H: 33 cm   Ø: 14 cm

Louis Comfort Tiffany

Born and died in New York (1848-1933). His father, Charles Lewis Tiffany (1812-1901), opened up a shop for luxury articles in New York in 1837. The shop soon developed into a world-famous jewellery workshop, known since 1853 as "Tiffany & Co." Louis Comfort Tiffany grew up in a cultured upper-class milieu, surrounded as a child by objects of artistic beauty. His father expected him to take over the jewellery business, but as an eighteen-year-old, Louis decided he wanted to be a painter. From 1864 to 1869 he travelled through France, England, North Africa and Spain. He was influenced by Moorish exoticism and was drawn towards the Oriental models valued by Parisian art dealers of the time. He visited Cairo and subsequently exhibited work at a number of exhibitions in the States. In 1871 his work was accepted by the National Academy. He married, for the first time, in 1872. In 1877 he founded the Society of American Artists and took part, in the same year, in the World Exhibition in Paris, where he showed two works. His interests turned more and more to the applied arts. In the same year he designed and made his first glass window. He founded, in 1879, together with Colman and de Forest, the Louis Comfort Tiffany Company of Associated Artists and took in the applied artist Candace Wheeler as a fourth partner.

The quartet worked together until 1883 in the sphere of interior design. Tiffany began to experiment with glass. In collaboration with John La Farge, he made technical and chemical experiments in the Heidt glassworks in Brooklyn. He developed, thereby, various methods for producing coloured and striped glass and eventually discovered the iridescent glass which he later named "Favrile" (Latin: *fabriles* = handmade). He was commissioned to design the interior decorations for the White House in Washington in 1882. His wife Mary died in 1884. A year later, in 1885, he founded the "Tiffany Glass Company", which was principally involved in manufacturing windows and items of interior design. His windows became increasingly well known, and were included in designs for hotels, clubhouses, villas, churches and theatres.

Tiffany was enthusiastic about electricity and the new problems and possibilities it presented in terms of lighting. Along with Thomas Edison, he designed the interior fittings for the Lyceum Theatre in New York, the first electrically lit theatre. In 1886 he married for the second time. In 1889 followed a further European tour, one of the products of which was the large window, *The Four Seasons*, which Tiffany sent to the World Exhibition of 1890 in Paris. This window was made out of a mosaic of irregular cabochons, whose rough surface produced special effects of light refraction. The combination of iridescence, semi-opaque effects and powerful shades is unique to this piece of work. As a result of this exhibition, Tiffany received commissions from the French artists Bonnard, Vuillard and Toulouse-Lautrec.

In 1892 he founded the Tiffany Glass and Decorating Company in New York. He exhibited the new firm's first lamps in Chicago in 1893 and was awarded fifty-four prizes! Simultaneously, in 1892/93, the Tiffany Furnaces, with their own refineries, were founded in Corona, Long Island. Opaline glass was made there for incorporation into windows and lamps and, after the end of 1893, also blown glass, made under the direction of Arthur J. Nash (1849-1934), though Louis C. Tiffany controlled the production.

In 1894 the Musée des Arts Décoratifs in Paris bought the first Tiffany goblet. In the same year the term "Favrile" was entered as a registered trademark. The first exhibition of Favrile glass followed in 1896. The art collector Havemeyer donated fifty-six of the most beautiful Favrile pieces to the Metropolitan Museum in New York. The first lamp catalogue appeared in 1898. In 1889 Samuel Bing, Tiffany's European representative, organized a large exhibition of his work in London. Tiffany changed the name of his firm to "Tiffany Studios" around 1900. The Paris World Exhibition of 1900 was a phenomenal success for Tiffany. His lamps were the sensation of the whole exhibition. The *Dragonfly Lamp*, designed by his colleague Clara Driscoll, was awarded the Grand Prix.

Tiffany's father died in 1902. Louis Tiffany now controlled almost unlimited capital. He was president of the Tiffany Studios and artistic director of the jewellery firm of Tiffany & Co. At the World Exhibition in Turin, his *Lily Lamp* was awarded the Grand Prix. In St Louis in 1904 he exhibited, for the first time, ceramics, enamel work and jewellery made to his own designs, and was awarded the gold medal. His second wife died in the same year. The famous huge mosaic-glass proscenium curtain was made in 1911 for the National Theatre in Mexico City. In 1915 the large glass mosaic picture, *Dream Garden*, which Tiffany designed, was built into the publishing house of Curtis Publishing Company in Philadelphia.

Between 1913 and 1916 Tiffany organized large parties which created a sensation. In 1919 Tiffany and Nash withdrew from taking an active part in the Tiffany Studios and the Tiffany Studios and Tiffany Furnaces Inc. were separated. A. D. Nash, a son of A. J. Nash, became director of the Tiffany Furnaces Inc., and Joseph Briggs took over the Studios. He inherited, therewith, a fabulous inventory of glass and bronze objects. After 1918 no lamp bases, lampshades, candlesticks or other accessories were signed with the "Tiffany Studios, New York" stamp. The Tiffany Furnaces Inc. continued operating until 1928, before Louis Comfort Tiffany withdrew his financial support and forbade the use of his name in the venture. The Tiffany Studios declared bankruptcy in 1932. A year later, Louis Comfort Tiffany died. At the time of his death, the worldwide recession of the thirties was at its peak, and America was flooded by the products of his workshops. In 1946, when Tiffany's name was almost forgotten, his private collection was auctioned off.

Robert Koch, the expert on Tiffany and his biographer, writes that renewed interest in Tiffany and the later enthusiasm for the Jugendstil were just beginning to make themselves felt at that time. This development was first noticed in Tiffany vases. The value of these unique pieces rose a hundredfold in the two decades which followed the Second World War. "Today the value of Tiffany lamps has not only caught up with that of the vases but has left it far behind. Fortunately this process did not happen indiscriminately, and more and more art critics share Samuel Bing's view that the works of art which Tiffany made out of free-blown glass break the boundaries of the 'Jugendstil' and reach the peak of pure art" (Robert Koch). Since the Tiffany Studios employed about two hundred craftsmen around 1905, Bing reported: "For Tiffany there was only one way to bring about a complete harmony between the various working methods in the arts and crafts. An enormous workshop under whose roof everything was combined: glass-blowers, stone setters, silversmiths and bronze casters, gilders, jewellers and model – makers all working together, all governed by the same ideal – to translate the ideas of a group of free-working artists into reality."

Tiffany himself made sure that in his studios only objects of the highest quality were produced, regardless of the cost. Only the purest bronze was good enough for his lamp bases and candlesticks. The mosaic lampshades were mounted in copper-foil and copper solder. Each separate piece was finished by hand and joined together with the greatest precision. Tiffany expected every craftsman he employed to be proud of his trade; and as long as he controlled the production, there was no room for rationalization or economy measures.

Robert Koch confirmed in a conversation we had, that there are many Tiffany lamps which bear no signature. A quantity of these lamps were ordered directly from him by the purchasers, who often expressed the desire that he should not imprint the maker's name into the metal. In these cases a metal tab was attached to the object, which bore the "Tiffany Studios, New York" mark and the model number. Such metal tabs or paper-label substitutes were mostly removed as being superfluous. As with other important works of art, the origin in these cases can easily be determined by the style and the overall quality.

The imitations which one sees on the market

today and which bear, unauthorized, the name of Louis Comfort Tiffany, are poor attempts to copy a style which disappeared with the death of this great craftsman.

377 *Hanging lamp*
White Dogwood. Favrile glass and opaline. Rim, finial and chain in bronze. As with all Tiffany lamps, the mosaic parts are assembled with copper solder.
~ 1903
Shade: Sign. Tiffany Studios, New York
⌀: 72 cm

378 *Hanging lamp*
Blue Daffodil. Daffodils with green leaves on a dark-blue ground. Tiffany opaline and Favrile glass. Hanging attachment with a bronze chain (fish design, Tiffany Studios). As with many commissioned Tiffany lamps, not signed.
~ 1906
⌀: 51 cm
Lit. Dr Egon Neustadt, *The Lamps of Tiffany* (identical example), p. 107, Ill. No. 155.
Robert Koch, *Louis C. Tiffany's Glass, Bronzes, Lamps*, p. 175, No. 615 (of the price list) "Hanging shades" (1906).

379 *Hanging lamp*
Burnt-Gold Laburnum. Bronze finial with hooks for the chain.
1904
Sign. Tiffany Studios, New York 1537
⌀: 53 cm

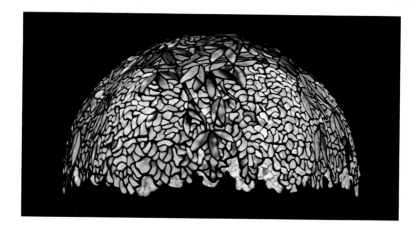

380 *Floor-lamp*
Magnolia. The opaline flowers are in relief; the calyces are in Favrile glass. Areas of the shade are backed with pea-sized glass pieces to create special light-effects.
1902
Sign. (Shade and base) Tiffany Studios, New York 1509
H: 194 cm   ⌀: 68 cm

381 *Floor-lamp*
Yellow and green Favrile glass. Geometric design. An extended bronze finial and a bronze foot.
1902
Sign. (Shade and base) Tiffany Studios, New York
H: 195 cm   ⌀: 62 cm

382 *Floor-lamp*
Peony Flower Border. The peony was Tiffany's favourite flower and a constant source of inspiration. The blooms are red, blending into pink, with orange-yellow centres, the flower-stems greenish brown; the leaves are in relief. The upper part of the shade is chartreuse-green opaline. The bronze finial has an elongated upper section.
~ 1902
Sign. (Shade and base) Tiffany Studios, New York 1574
H: 194 cm   ⌀: 59 cm

383   Floor-lamp
Dogwood Flower Belt. Tiffany
opaline and Favrile glass in
yellow, pink and green on a green
patinated base. The shade is set in
an adjustable frame.
~ 1902
Sign. (Shade) Tiffany Studios,
New York
Sign. (Base) Tiffany Studios, New
York 682
H: 142 cm   ∅: 25 cm
Lit. Dr Egon Neustadt, *The Lamps
of Tiffany*, p. 82, Ill. No. 115; p. 34,
Ill. Nos. 29/30

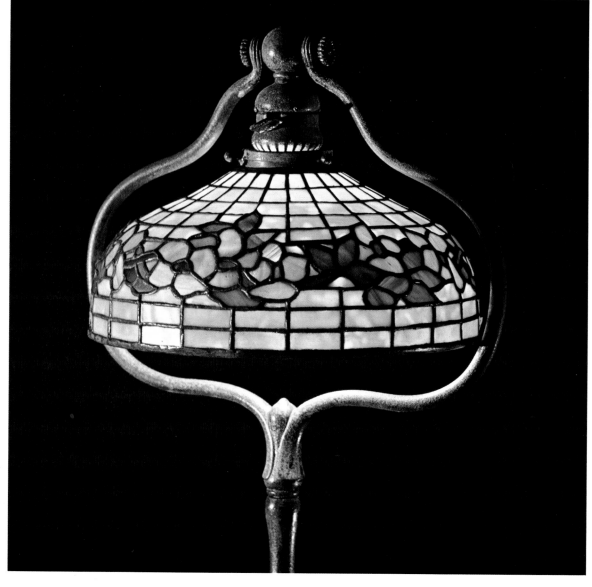

384   Floor-lamp
Geometric pattern in green,
white, yellow and gold. A mosaic
of opaline and Favrile glass. The
lower border of the shade is made
up of narrow rectangular pieces
arranged vertically. Turkish
finial. The richly decorated
bronze base has a particularly
beautiful patina.
1902
Sign. (Shade and base) Tiffany
Studios, New York
H: 210 cm   ∅: 68 cm

385   Floor-lamp
Poinsettia. Colours: white, red,
green, yellow, blue and violet.
The flower stamens are in bronze
filigree. Gilt-bronze base with a
swivel-arm and a spherical
counterweight.
~ 1900
Sign. Tiffany Studios, New York
H (Base): 125 cm
W (Swivel-arm): 37 cm
H (Shade): 15 cm   ∅: 24.5 cm

386 Table-lamp
Light-Blue Miniature Wisteria.
The construction is the same as in
the large Wistaria lamps, except
that the base is bronze with a dark
patina. The glass mosaic pieces
are also proportionally a little
larger than in the big table-lamps.
1900
Sign. (Shade and base) Tiffany
Studios, New York
H: 45 cm Ø: 25 cm

387 Table-lamp
Red-Bodied Dragonfly. Tiffany
opaline and Favrile glass; the
etched bronze wings are on an
emerald green and yellowish
ground, set with jewelled-glass
cabochons. Stands on a bronze
base with four feet. Louis C.
Tiffany was awarded the Grand
Prix in 1900 at the World
Exhibition for this design.
(Designed by Clara Driscoll.)
1900
Sign. (Shade) Tiffany Studios,
New York 1495
Sign. (Base) Tiffany Studios, New
York 364
H: 67.5 cm Ø: 50 cm
Lit. Dr Egon Neustadt, *The Lamps
of Tiffany*, pp. 102-03, Ill. No. 149

388 *Table-lamp*
Summer Peony. With leaves on a
sapphire-blue ground. Opaline
and Favrile glass set in gilded
copper, mounted on a gilded
bronze foot.
~ 1900
Sign. (Base) Tiffany Studios, New
York
H: 60 cm ∅: 44.5 cm

389 *Table-lamp*
Geometric Flower. Design of
stylized leaves in blue-green
Favrile glass intersected with
honey-yellow; crown and border
decorated with severe geometric
shapes. Mounted on a gilt-bronze
foot.
~ 1910
Sign. (Shade) Tiffany Studios,
New York 1474
Sign. (Base) Tiffany Studios, New
York 528
H: 68 cm ∅: 46 cm

390 *Table-lamp*
Blue-Bodied Dragonfly. The shade is yellow Favrile opaline glass with round jewel glass in the dragonfly border. The base, which is especially beautiful, has an inlay of Favrile glass mosaic and gilded-bronze dragonflies, with a spiral of mosaic winding up the stem.
1900
Sign. Tiffany Studios, New York
H: 47 cm   Ø: 34 cm
Lit. Victor Arwas, *Glass Art Nouveau to Art Deco*, p. 216

391 *Table-lamp*
Cherry Tree on Green. Stylized representation of a cherry tree, with blossom, leaves and fruit. The dark patina of the tree-trunk and roots spreads out into the branches on the crown of the shade and these are continued down the curve of the shade as dark opaline.
~ 1900
Marked: (Shade) 347/1
Sign. (Base) Tiffany Studios, New York 9919
H: 67 cm   Ø: 47 cm

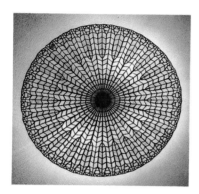

392   Table-lamp
Blue-White Wisteria. The bronze base represents the trunk with roots, which branches out at the top of the lamp into boughs, the top parts of which are not set with glass. The branches stretch down into the bottom third of the shade in places. The white, green, yellow and blue mosaic of opaline forms the clusters of wisteria flowers and the irregular lower border follows the flow of the blooms. (Designed by Curtis Freshel.)
~ 1900
Sign. (Shade and base) Tiffany Studios, New York 1073
H: 83 cm   ∅: 47 cm

393   Table-lamp
Green Lotus Leaf. Geometrically arranged, slightly stylized lotus leaves form a wavy pattern on the shade, which has a reflexed edge. The spectrum of colours in the opaline ranges from dark blue, through green and various shades of yellow, to almost white. Base and finial are bronze. The shade has more than 1,300 mosaic pieces.
1904
Sign. (Shade) Tiffany Studios, New York
Sign. (Base) Tiffany Studios, New York 1524
H: 74 cm   ∅: 66 cm

394   Table-lamp
White Dream. Favrile glass in mother-of-pearl, gold and silver-blue. This extremely rare design, composed of hundreds of carefully matched glass segments, shines even without illumination. The fine copper solder is gilded throughout. Gilt-bronze base.
1907
Sign. (Shade) Tiffany Studios, New York 1913
Sign. (Base) Tiffany Studios, New York 533
On the electric fitting: 1907
H: 54 cm   ∅: 46 cm
Lit. Dr Egon Neustadt, *The Lamps of Tiffany*, p. 60; Robert Koch, *Louis C. Tiffany's Glass, Bronzes, Lamps*, p. 194, Ill. No. 33

395 *Table-lamp*
Red-Purple-White Poppy. The petals are made of textured glass. The pollen and the veins of the leaves are represented by additions of filigree bronze. An abstract design, echoing that of the shade, covers the whole of the illuminated green opaline base, which stands on four claws.
1900
Sign. (Shade) Tiffany Studios, New York 531
Sign. (Base) Tiffany Studios, New York 002
H: 69 cm   Ø: 51.5 cm
Base area: 18.5 x 18.5 cm

396 *Table-lamp*
Bellflower. Opaline. Triple composition of yellowish and reddish bellflowers with leaves. Vase-shaped bronze foot with a dark-brown patina on a quadrangular base.
~ 1900
Sign. (Shade) Tiffany Studios, New York;
(Base) monogram and label: Tiffany Studios, New York 444
H: 48 cm   Ø: 41 cm

398   *Table-lamp*
Pink Geranium. Favrile opaline,
representing flowering
geraniums; with a greenish
patina on the bronze base.
H: 57 cm   ∅: 42.5 cm
Lit. Dr Egon Neustadt, *The Lamps
of Tiffany*, p. 95, Ill. No. 136

397   *Table-lamp*
Dogwood Flower Belt. Tiffany
opaline in green, white, gold and
yellow. Flowers and leaves on a
green ground. The telescopic
bronze base has four feet.
~ 1900
Sign (Shade) Tiffany Studios,
New York 1553
Sign. (Base) Tiffany Studios, New
York 440
H: 58 cm   ∅: 35.5 cm
Lit. Dr Egon Neustadt, *The Lamps
of Tiffany*, p. 82, Ill. No. 115

399 *Floor-lamp*
Autumn Leaves. Spherical shade in a particularly beautiful opaline, with copper-solder mount.
Design: autumn foliage in varied colours ranging from yellowish green to dark red. The polished bronze foot has a relief pattern of overlapping artichoke leaves.
Sign. (inside shade and on base plate (not illustrated) Tiffany Studios, New York
H: 80 cm
⌀: 25.5 cm

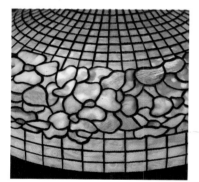

400 *Table-lamp*
Dogwood Flower Belt. A garland of dogwood flowers encircles the shade, on a ground that is yellowish green at the base, merging into dark green at the top. The bronze finial and foot have a dark-brown patina.
~ 1900
Sign. (Shade) Tiffany Studios, New York
Sign. (Base) Tiffany Studios, New York 528
H: 75 cm   ⌀: 52 cm

401 *Table-lamp*
Green Turtleback. The green Favrile opaline is decorated with a band of thick, stone-like glass resembling turtleshell.
Bronze base on four feet with a geometric design. Extendable shaft.
1900
Sign. (Shade and base) Tiffany Studios, New York
H: 81 cm   ⌀: 59 cm

402 *Table-lamp*
Flowering Lotus. The bronze
platform consists of carved
water-lily leaves rising up to form
a thick base for the stem which
consists of eight stalks. The shade
is bell-shaped, indented at the
top, and represents a curtain of
stems on a blue Favrile opaline
ground, ending in the lotus
flowers which form the irregular
border.
~ 1902
Sign. Tiffany Studios, New York
H: 65.5 cm   Ø: 46 cm

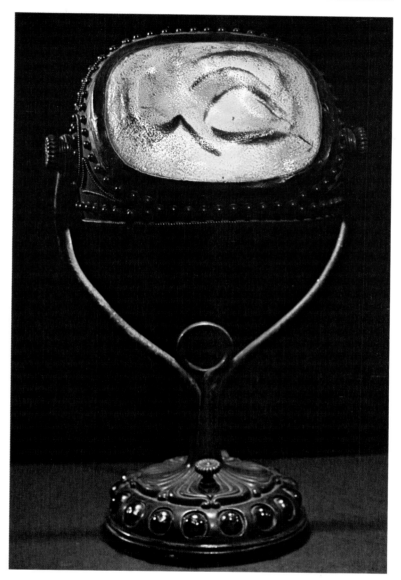

403 *Writing-desk lamp*
Turtleback Swivel. Tiffany
jewelled glass, both inside and
out. Colours: (unlit) darkly
iridescent shades of purple, blue
and amber; (illuminated) shining
emerald green and gold. The
shade swivels in its bronze frame.
Inset in the heavy circular bronze
base are large jewel-glass pearls.
1900/1901
Sign. (Base) Tiffany Studios, New
York 408-9048
H: 36.5 cm
Lit. Dr Egon Neustadt, *The Lamps
of Tiffany*, p. 55, Ill. No. 70

408 *Small table-lamp*
Bronze base on nine small feet.
Shade of blown Favrile glass with
a geometric etched design.
1902
Sign. (Shade and base) Tiffany
Studios, New York
H: 50 cm   ∅: 26 cm

404 *Small lamp*
A three-branched bronze base
supports the blown gold-
coloured Favrile glass dome with
a feather design.
1908
Sign. (Base) Tiffany Studios, New
York 445
H: 42 cm   ∅: 25 cm

405 *Small lamp*
Blown Favrile glass shade with a
wavy design, on a bronze base
and frame. Colours: green and
gold.
~ 1908
Sign. (Shade) L. C. T.
Sign. (Base) Tiffany Studios, New
York
H: 34 cm   ∅: 18 cm

406 *Small lamp*
Iridescent Favrile glass in gold,
green and blue. Adapted for
electricity, oil or candle.
1910
Sign. L. C. T.
H: 33 cm

407 *Writing-desk lamp*
Bronze carved with the zodiac
signs of the Lion, Ram and Bull.
Sign. Tiffany Studios, New York
414
H: 23 cm   W: 28 cm
Lit. Robert Koch, *Louis C.
Tiffany's Glass, Bronzes, Lamps*,
p. 193, Ill. No. 18

409 *Table-lamp*
Lily Lamp. Gilt-bronze base with
lily pads and buds. Blown Favrile
glass shades representing the lily
flowers. Each of the eighteen
shades is signed L. C. T. There
are Lily Lamps with 3, 6, 10, 12
and 18 blooms, used as small
lamps, table-lamps and floor-
lamps.
1898
Marked (Base) Tiffany Studios,
New York 1063
An identical model with a base in
dark-brown patina in Hamburg,
privately owned.

411 *Table-lamp*
Clematis. Favrile opaline in light green, green, pink, purple and light brown. Design: a garland of variously coloured flowering clematis with leaves. Bronze base with green-brown patina.
1905
Sign. (Shade) Tiffany Studios, New York 489
Sign. (Base) Tiffany Studios, New York 533
H: 57.5 cm   Ø: 45.5 cm

410 *Table-lamp*
Golden Acorn. Golden-yellow Favrile opaline with a floral garland of variously coloured gleaming opaline. Bronze foot on a round plate; six curved claws supporting the stem.
1905
Sign. (Shade) Tiffany Studios, New York J 3 V 1215
Sign. (Base) Tiffany Studios, New York 611
H: 55 cm   Ø: 40.5 cm

412 *Lantern*
Bronze base, with a stylized swan's head as a handle. Candle holder in decorated Favrile glass. Shade in yellow-green Favrile glass with a feather design and eight indentations.
1899
Sign. (Base) Tiffany Studios, New York 1477-1203
H: 32 cm

413 *Candlestick*
Bronze base with candle nozzle enclosed in Favrile glass. Small shade in gold Favrile glass with a combed green design.
~ 1900
Sign. Tiffany Studios, New York
H: 48.5 cm
Lit. Victor Arwas, *Glass Art Nouveau to Art Deco*, p. 226

414 *Candlestick*
Round base plate and tall, slender stem. The nozzle is made of carved bronze filled in with Favrile glass.
1901
Sign. Tiffany Studios, New York
H: 44 cm
Lit. Victor Arwas, *Glass Art Nouveau to Art Deco*, p. 213

416 *Candlestick*
Patinated bronze.
~ 1900
Sign. Tiffany Studios, New York
H: 33 cm   W: 12 cm
Ill. R. Schmutzler, *Art Nouveau–Jugendstil*, p. 19

417 *Candlestick*
Favrile glass held in a bronze mount, on a round base plate.
1905
Sign. Tiffany Studios, New York
10063
H: 27 cm

415 *Pair of candlesticks*
Iridescent Favrile glass. Blue, gold, green and red.
1911
Sign. L. C. Tiffany – Inc. Favrile
H: 31 cm

418 *Table-lamp*
Orange-Red Poppy, with leaves.
Tiffany opaline and Favrile glass,
partly textured. The leaf-veins
are composed of filigree bronze
pieces laid behind the leaves on
the inside of the shade. The seed
pods are also of fine bronze
filigree, laid on the outside. The
bronze base has a particularly
beautiful brown-green patina.
This is one of the most beautiful
and important examples of
Tiffany craftsmanship in the Art
Nouveau period.
~ 1900
Sign. (Shade) Tiffany Studios,
New York 1461
Sign. (Base) Tiffany Studios, New
York 503
H: 51 cm   Ø: 41 cm
Lit. Dr Egon Neustadt, *The Lamps
of Tiffany,* p. 96, Ill. No. 137

Vineland Flint Glass Works

The story of this firm is closely linked with that of Victor Durand, who was born in Baccarat, France, in 1870. Durand's father, grandfather and great-grandfather all worked at the world-famous Cristallerie de Baccarat. Durand's career as a glassmaker began when he was twelve years old. In 1882 the family emigrated to the USA. For thirteen years Durand worked in a number of glassware firms in Pennsylvania, Ohio and Virginia, and also in Canada. Then, in 1897, he and his father took over the Vineland Glass Manufactory Company (already in existence) in Vineland. Victor Durand's dream was to make art glass. In 1924 he began a correspondence with Martin Bach Jr, the son of the famous Quezal glass manufacturer, Martin Bach, who had been unable to keep his father's business going, and Durand brought him over to Vineland. Durand Art Glass began to be produced in 1926. Bach attracted a number of qualified people who had at one time worked for Quezal, and their influence is apparent in the first years of production. Subsequently, new colours and new styles of Durand glass were developed. Vase-like, iridescent lamp bases and crystal chandeliers were made, as well as numerous blown, coloured lampshades, up until 1931, the year of Durand's death.

419 *Pair of small lamps*
Opal-gold lustre glass with a
peacock feather design.
1926
H: 33 cm   ∅: 11 cm
Lit. u. Revi, *American Art Nouveau
Glass*, p. 438, No. 2028

VIII Documentation for France
(from *Le Luminaire*)

AVIS AUX ARTISTES ET ARTISANS

Au Premier Octobre 1895 il sera ouvert dans les Galeries de Mr S. BING 22 Rue de Provence à Paris sous le titre

L'ART NOUVEAU

une Exposition permanente & internationale de toutes productions artistiques sans distinction de catégories.

Cette Exposition comprendra:

LA SCULPTURE, LA PEINTURE, LE DESSIN ET LA GRAVURE ; LES ARTS DU DÉCOR, DU MOBILIER ET DE L'OBJET UTILE.

Seront admises toutes les œuvres d'art qui manifesteront une conception personnelle en accord avec l'esprit moderne.

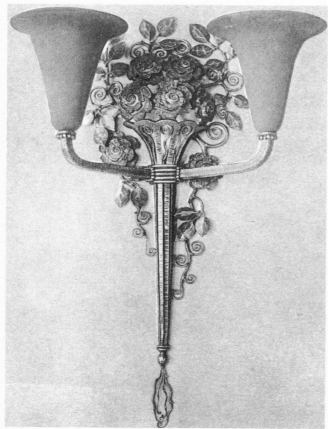

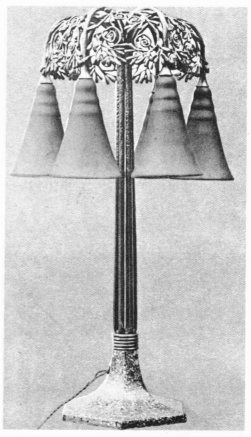

EDGAR BRANDT - Appliques. Lampe.

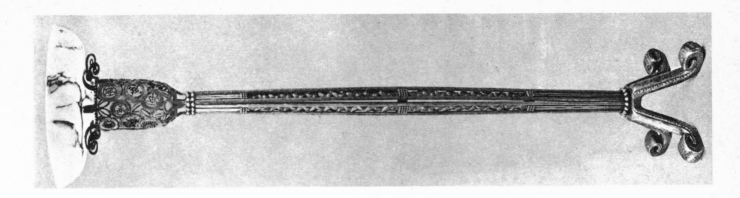

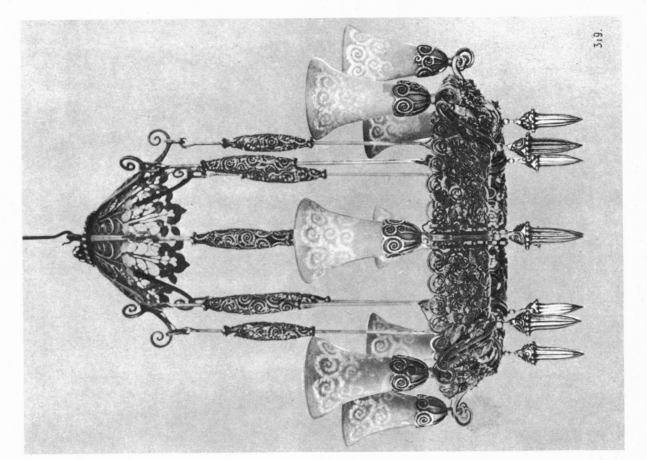

3.9.

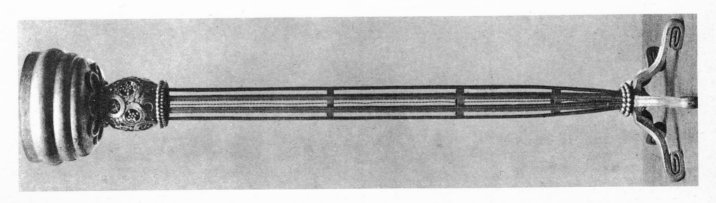

EDGAR BRANDT · Lustre. Torchères

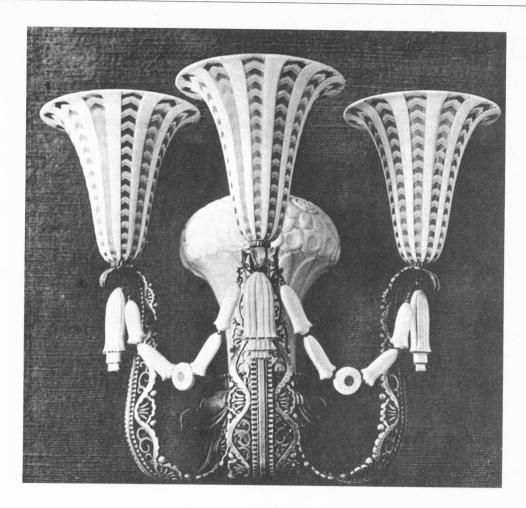

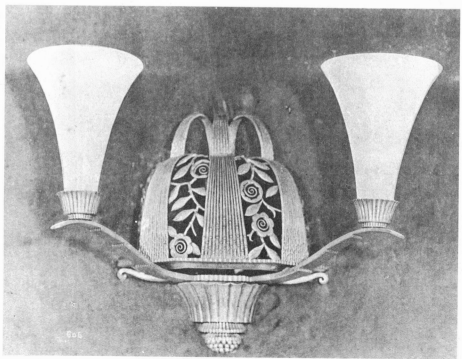

EDGAR BRANDT - Appliques.

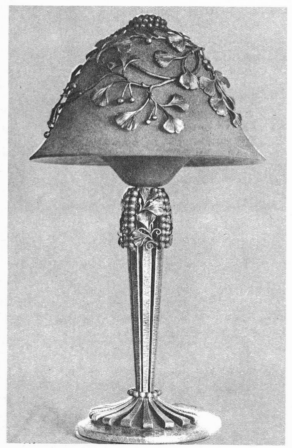

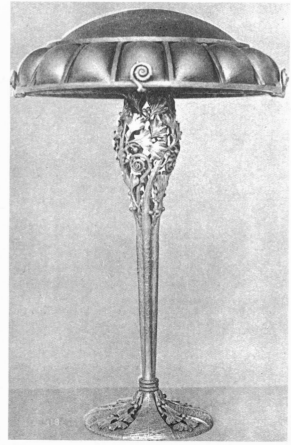

EDGAR BRANDT - Lustre. Lampes.

Desny

DESNY

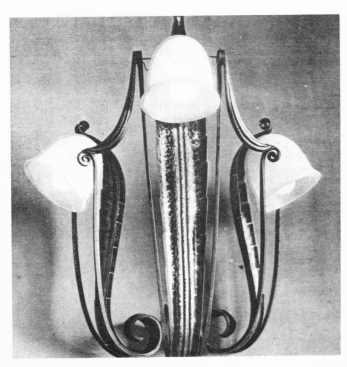

SUE & MARE

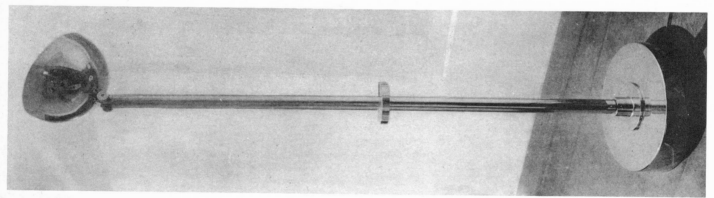

DESNY

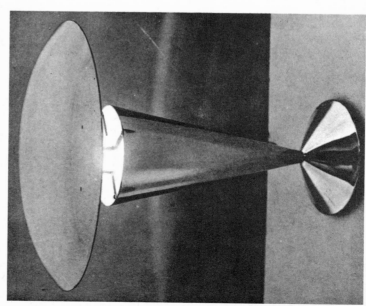

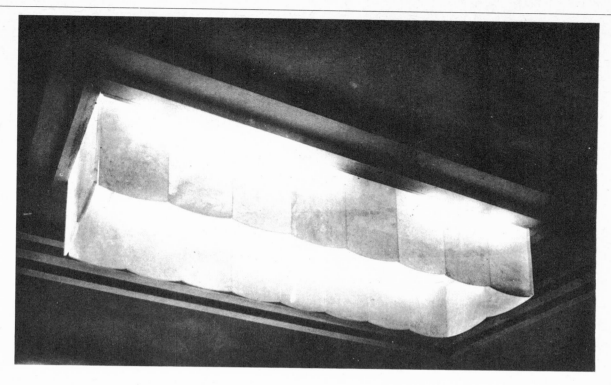

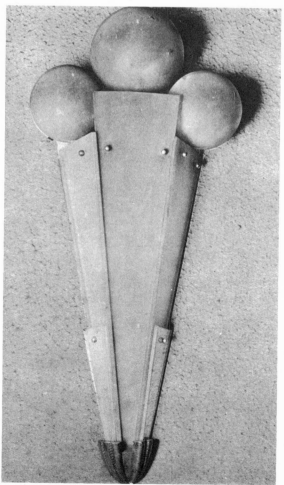

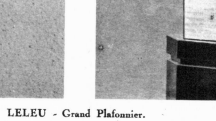

DILLY - Applique murale.   LELEU - Grand Plafonnier.   Paul HENNINGSEN - Lampe.

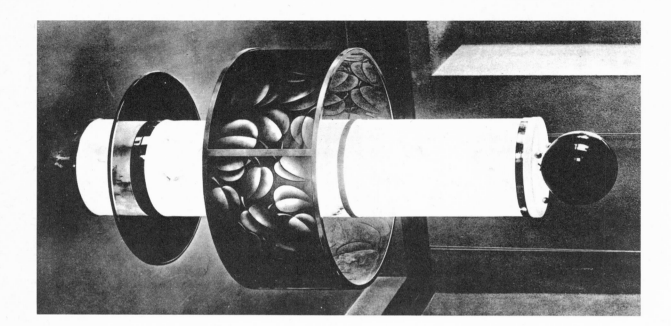

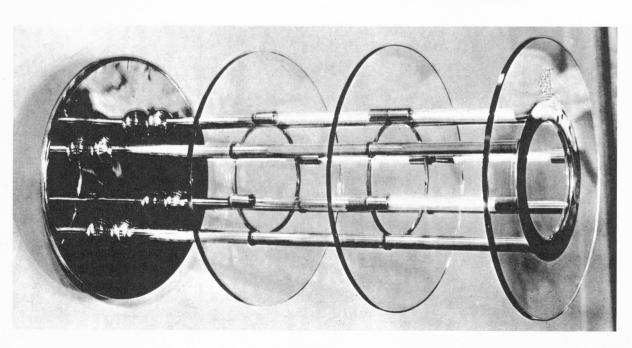

MAURICE DUFRÈNE

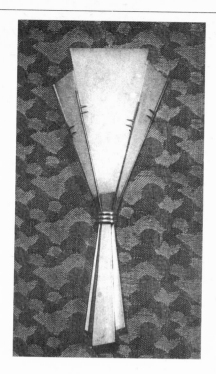

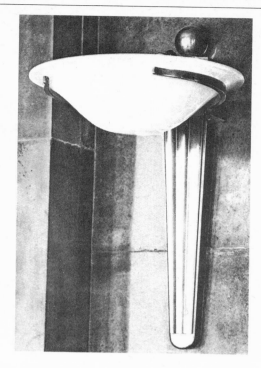

DOMINIQUE - Applique murale.　　　André GROULT - Bloc de cristal.　　　RUHLMANN - Applique murale.
RUHLMANN - Applique murale.　　　　　　　　　　　　　　　　　　　　　SUE & MARE - Applique murale.

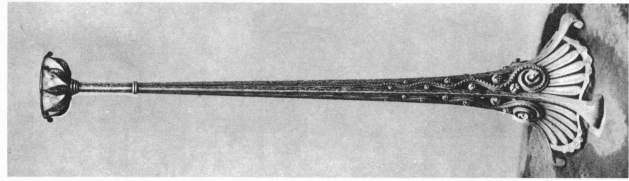

MALATRE & TONNELIER - Torchère

Paul FOLLOT & H. BOILEAU - Grand Plafonnier

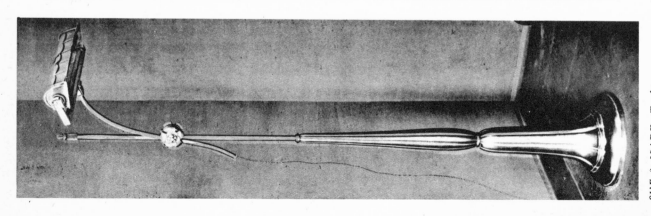

SUE & MARE - Torchère

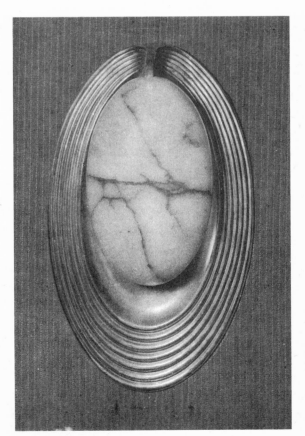

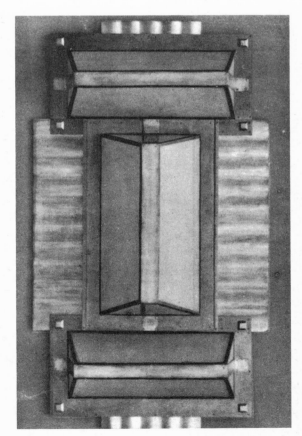

DOMINIQUE - Applique.   Paul FOLLOT - Lustre de salon.   René HERBST - Plafonnier.

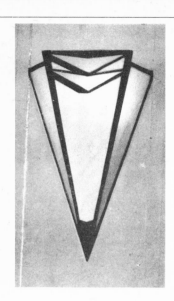

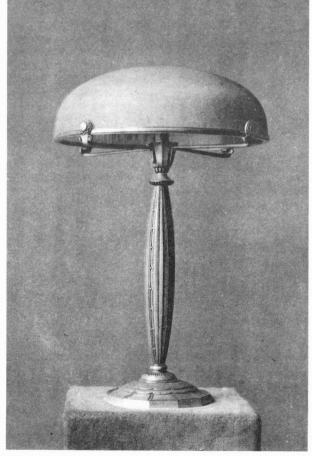

J. PERZEL - Lampe.   RUHLMANN - Applique.   J. PERZEL - Applique.

DUNAIME - Lampes bronze argenté.

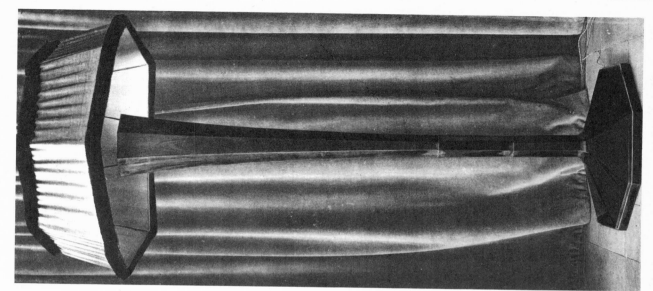

DOMINIQUE - Torchère.

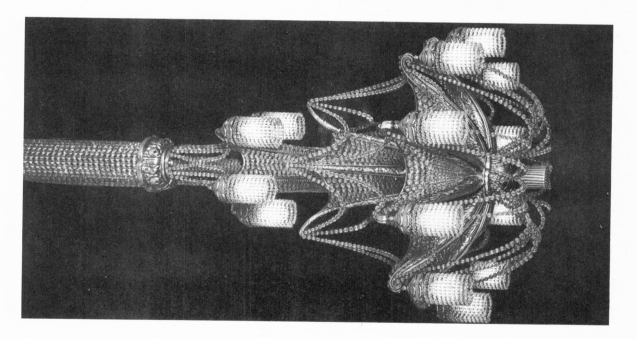

CHEVALIER - Lustre.

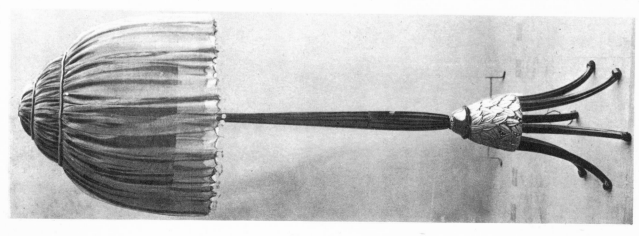

Paul FOLLOT - Torchère.

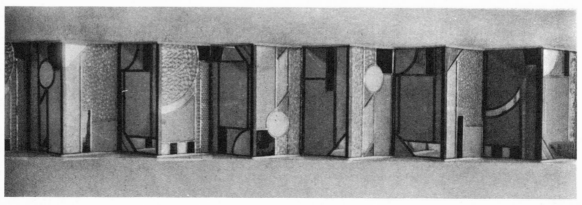

Maurice DUFRENE - Lustre.   MALLET-STEVENS - Plafond lumineux.   Simon GATE & Edward HOLD - Pendentif.

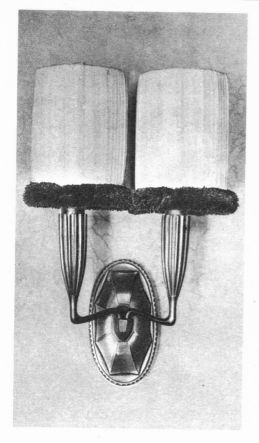
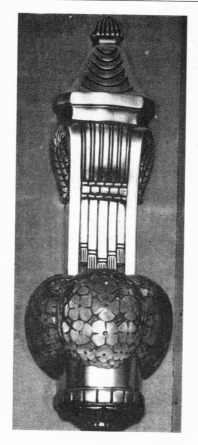
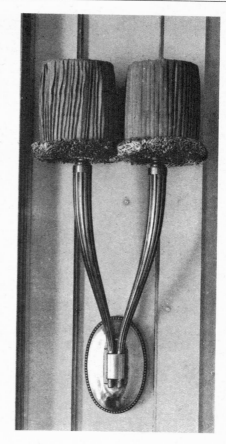

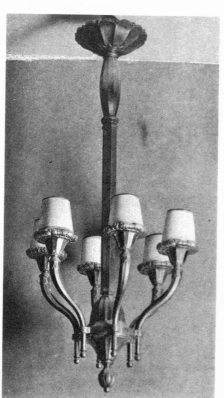

RUHLMANN - Applique.
GRANGER - Lustre.

SIMONET Frères - Applique.
GRANGER - Lustre.

RUHLMANN - Applique.
CAPON - Petit Lustre.

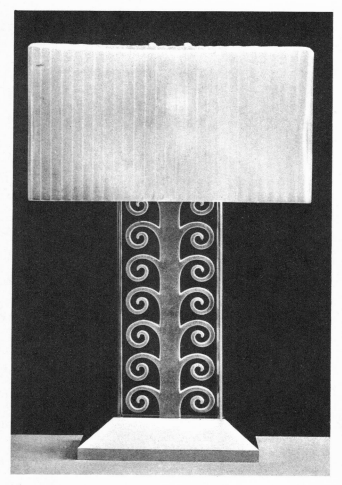 

LALIQUE

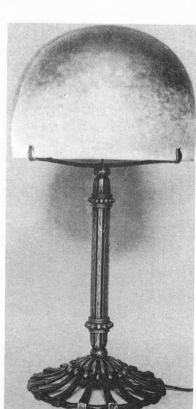

Raymond SUBES - Appliques. Lampes.

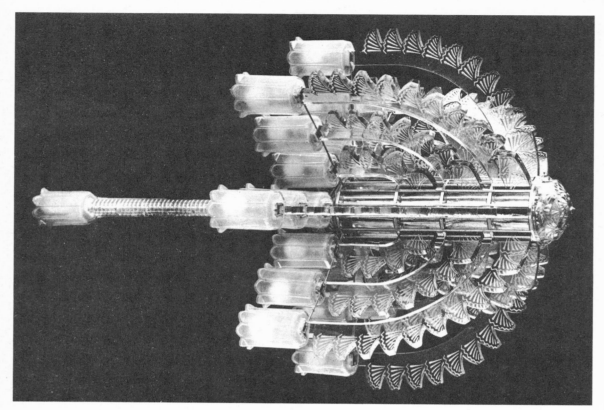

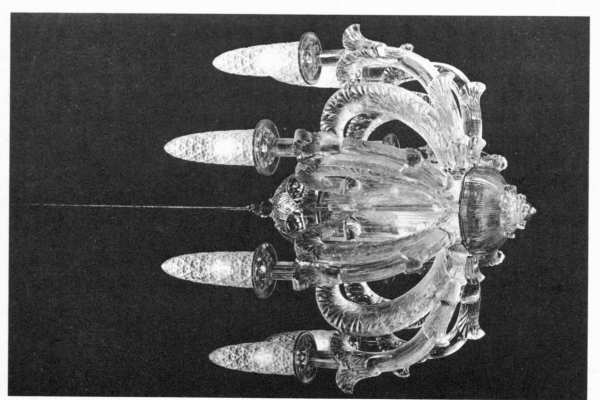

LALIQUE

213

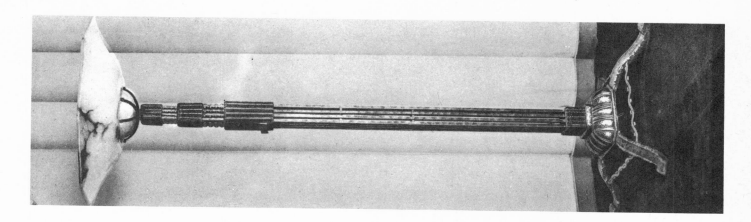

Raymond SUBES - Plafonnier. Applique. Torchères

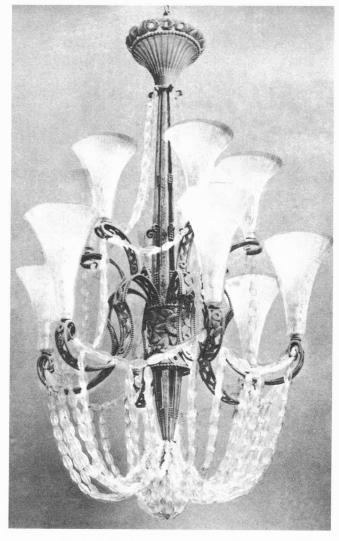

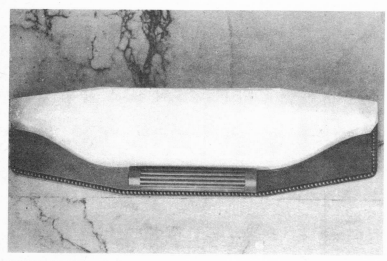

RUHLMANN - .Plafonnier.   **RUHLMANN** - Appliques.   **EDGAR BRANDT** - Lustre.

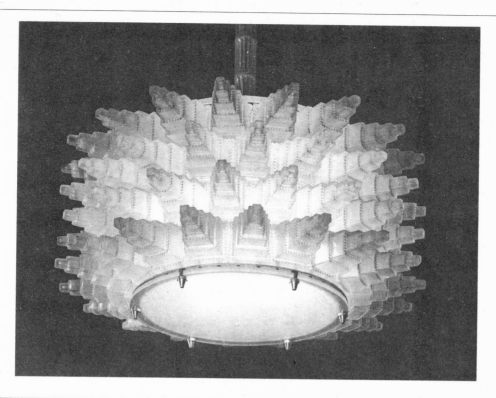

R. LALIQUE

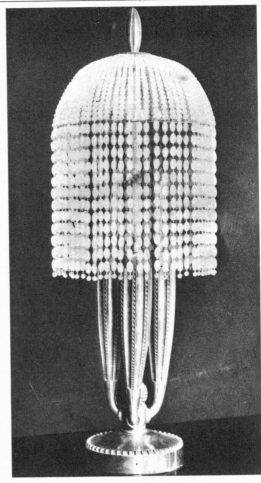

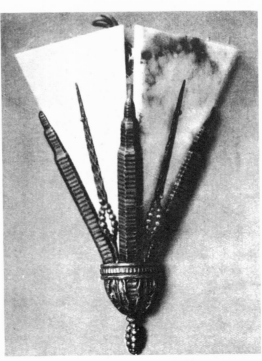

GENET & MICHON - Lustre.
Mlle MAISONNIER - Lustre.

RUHLMANN - Lampe.
Paul KISS - Applique.

JEAN PERZEL

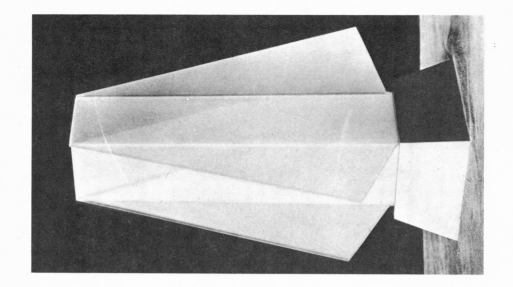

JEAN PERZEL

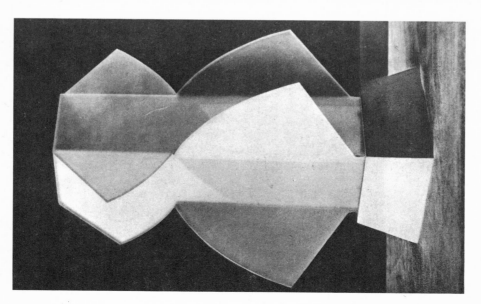

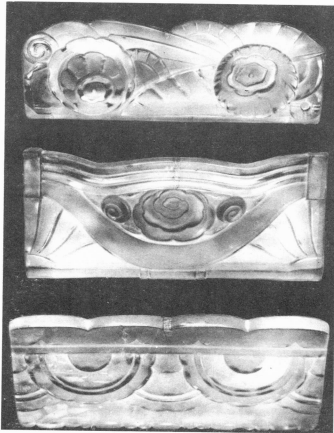

SABINO - Lustres. Plaques de verre. Lanterne.

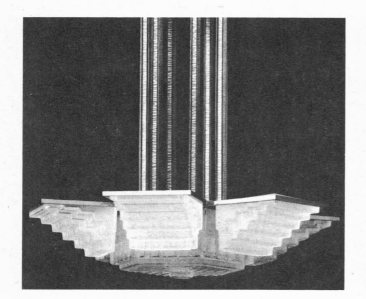

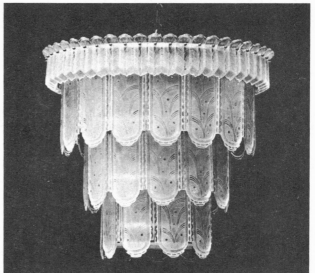

SABINO

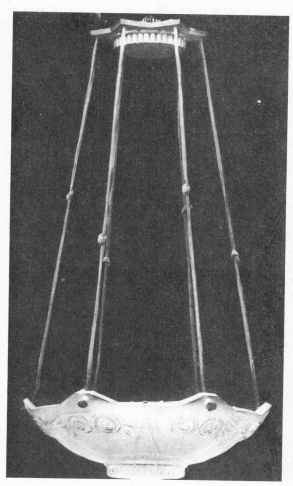

SABINO - Lustres

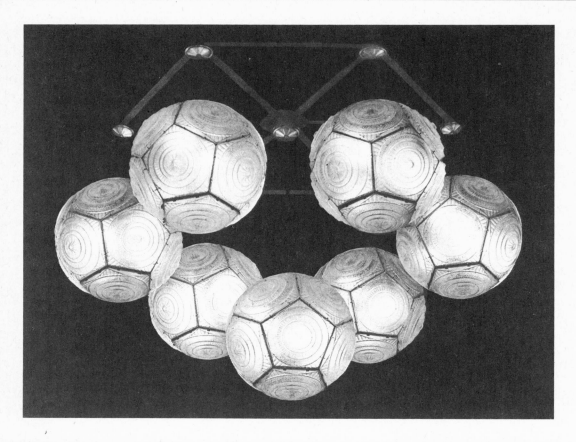

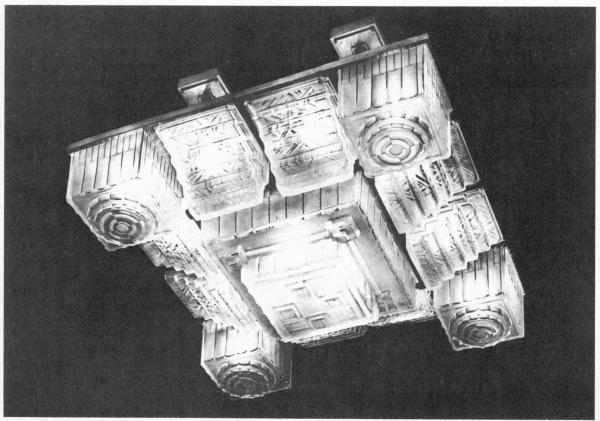

SABINO

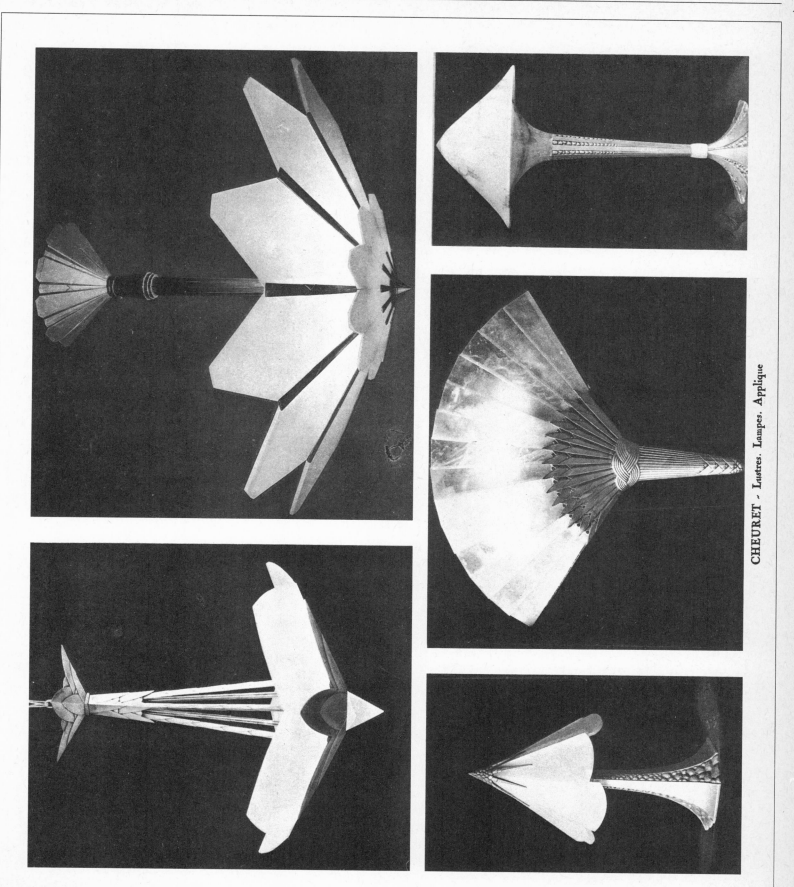

CHEURET ~ Lustres. Lampes. Applique

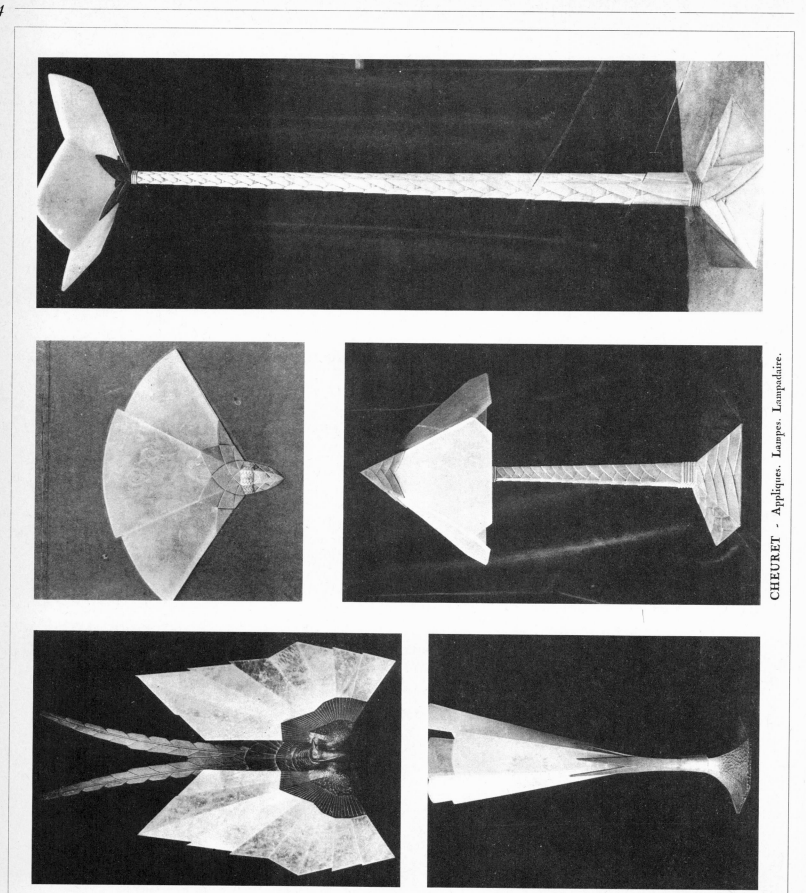

CHEURET - Appliques. Lampes. Lampadaire.

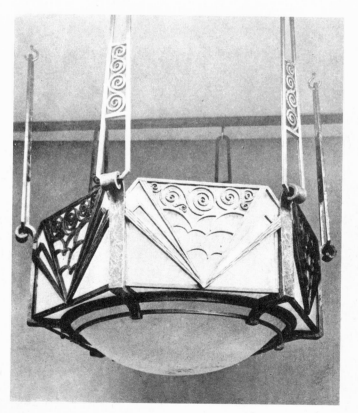

RAYMOND SUBES

226

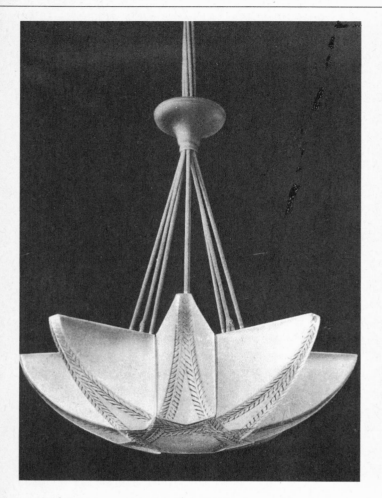

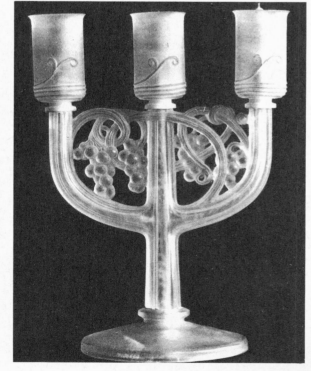

LALIQUE - Lustres. Poisson. Lampe.

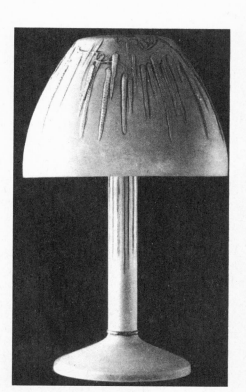

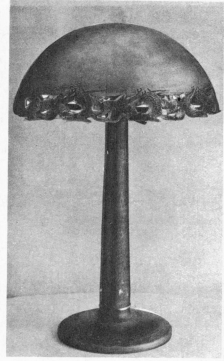

LALIQUE - Boule. Lustre. Lampes. Statuette.

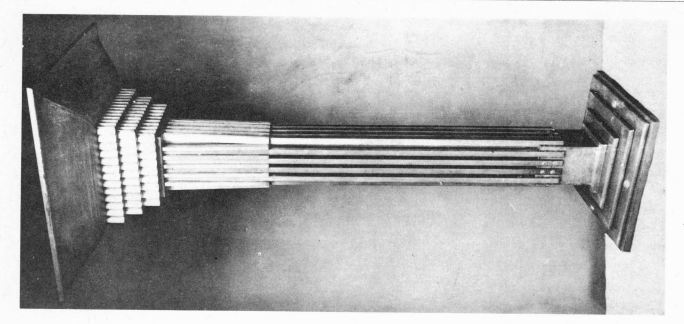

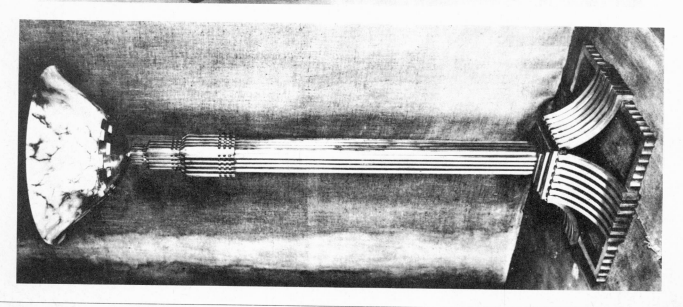

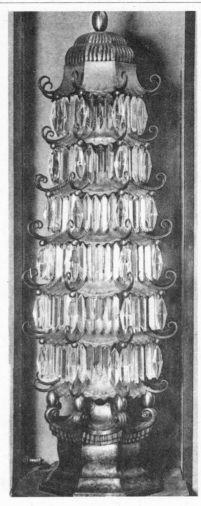

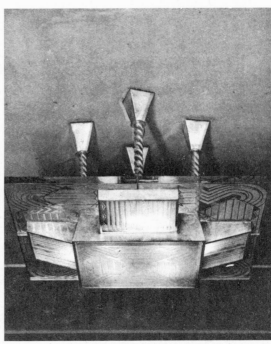

Paul **FOLLOT** - Grand Lustre.
DUCRET - Lampe.

SECTION SUISSE - Lampadaire.
KOHLMANN - Lustre.

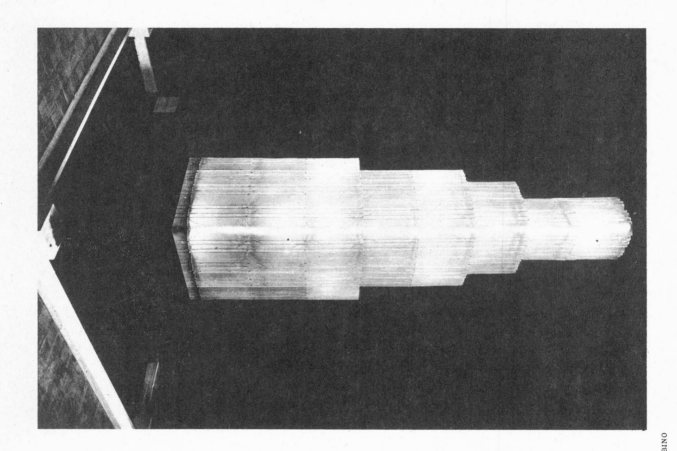

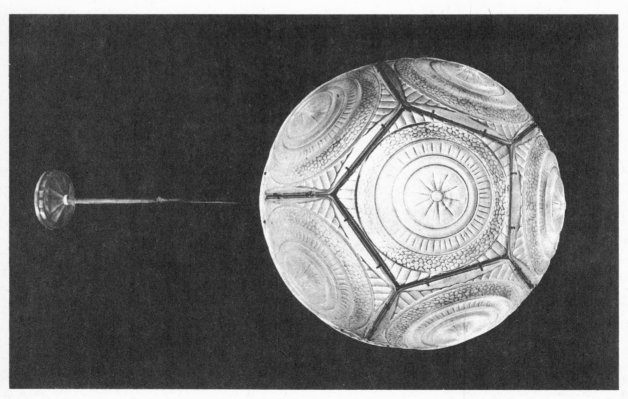

SABINO

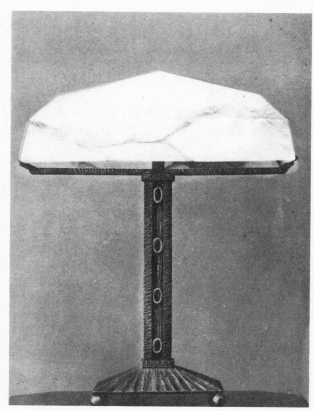

ART POPULAIRE POLONAIS - Plafonnier.
DOMINIQUE - Lampe de bureau.

René **PROU** - Petit Lustre.
Paul **FOLLOT** - Lampe de bureau.

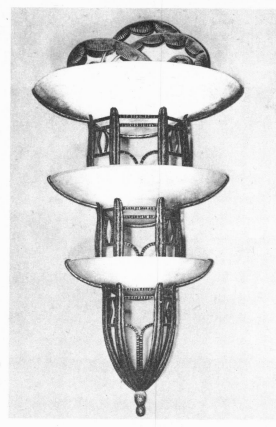

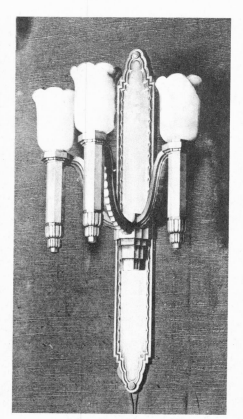

SIMONET Frères - Lustre.

GRANGER - Applique murale.   BOILEAU & SAUNIER DUVAL - Lanterne pendentif.

MORAND & Cie - Applique murale.

GRANGER - Applique murale.

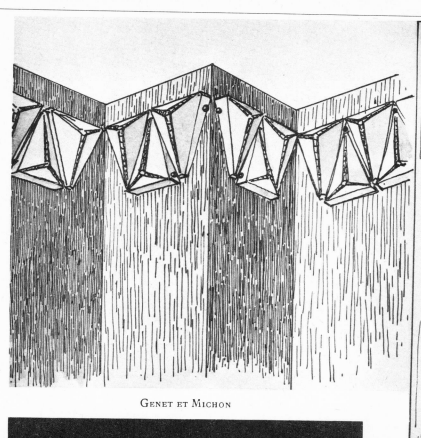

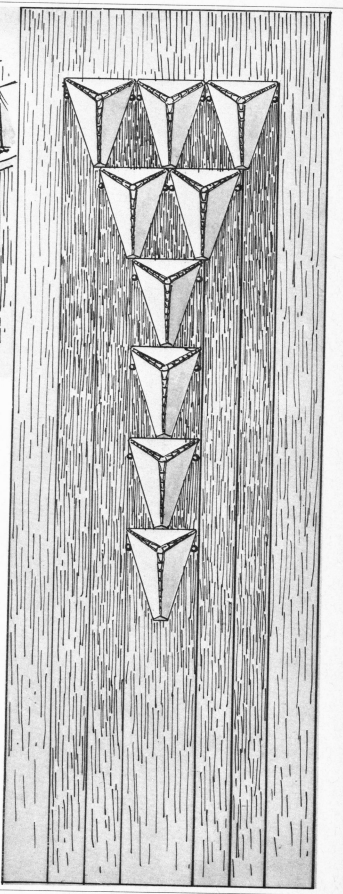

GENET ET MICHON

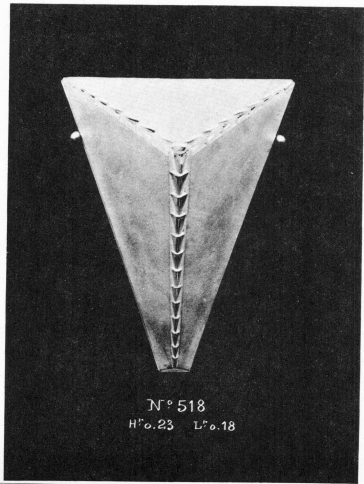

Nº 518

Hᵗ o.23   Lᵍ o.18

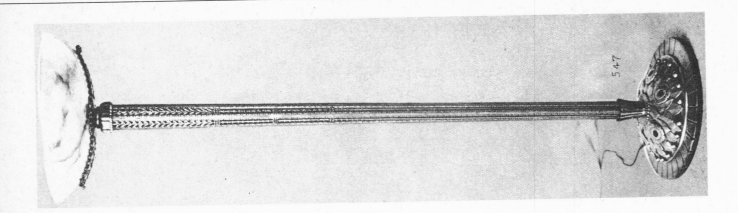

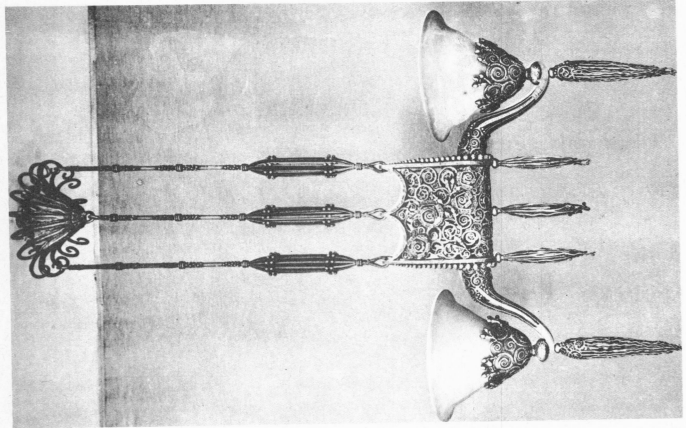

EDGAR BRANDT   Plafonnier. Torchères

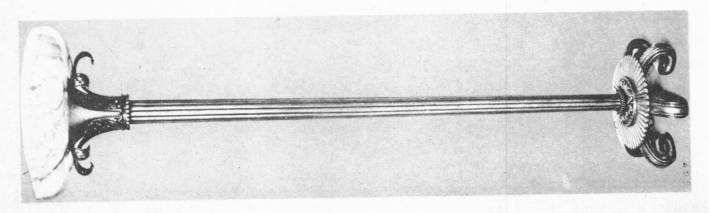

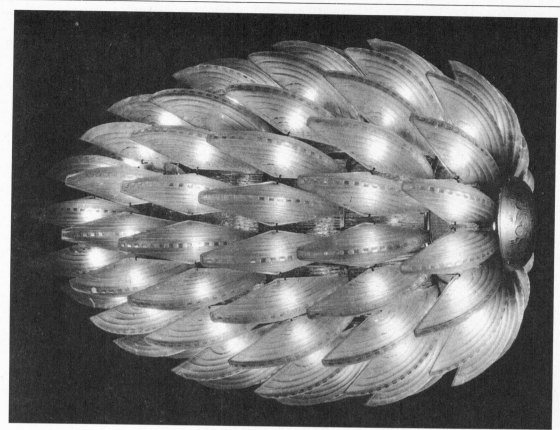

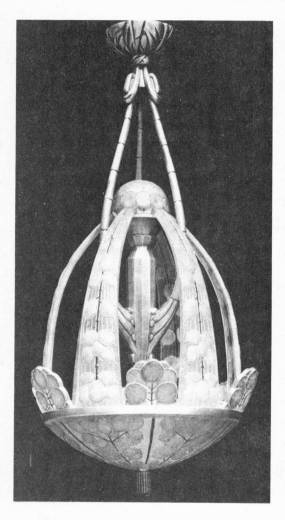

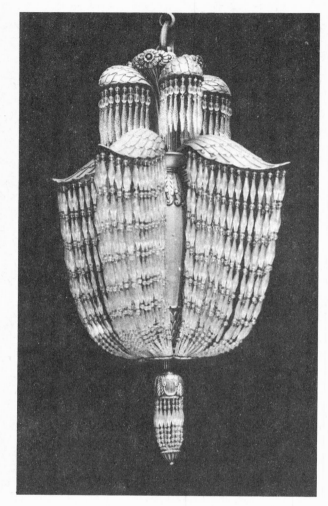

SIMONET Frères - Lustres. Appliques

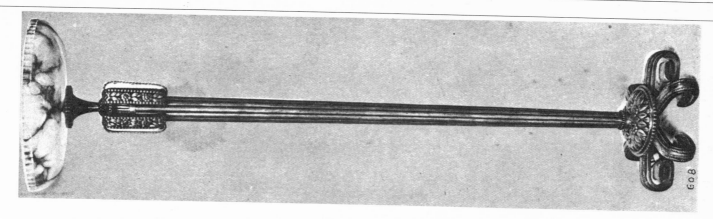

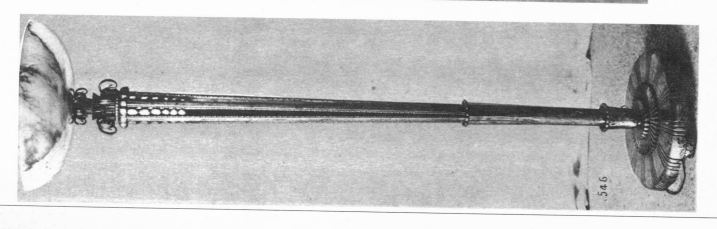

EDGAR BRANDT - Lustre. Torchères

– *Design & shapes for lamp shades and a complete vase-lamp from a catalog of The US Art Bent Glass Co., Hartford, Conn.*

24 Inch 1075

360

960

500

501

502

825

– Table lamps and hanging domes and light fixtures from the Moran & Manufacturing Co.'s 1912 catalog.

No. 10310—BRUSH BRASS

Length, 36 in.

Includes 18 in. art glass dome, body color No. 13, leaves No. 98, and purple grapes, unless otherwise specified.

	Not Wired	Wired	Complete No Lamps
1 Lt. Elec.	$33.00	$34.00	$34.40
2 Lt. Elec.	33.25	34.50	35.30
3 Lt. Elec.	33.50	35.00	36.20

Extra Lengthening, per foot

Not Wired.........$2.00   Wired.........$2.20

No. 10312—BRUSH BRASS
Length, 36 in.
Includes 24 in. art glass dome, colors No. 11 and No. 41, unless otherwise specified.

	Not Wired	Wired	Complete No Lamps
1 Lt. Elec.	$72.00	$73.00	$73.40
2 Lt. Elec.	72.25	73.50	74.30
3 Lt. Elec.	72.50	74.00	75.20
4 Lt. Elec.	72.75	74.50	76.10

Extra Lengthening, per foot
Not Wired.........$1.50   Wired.........$1.70

No. 10316—BRUSH BRASS
Length, 36 in.
Includes 18 in. bent art glass dome, color No. 98, unless otherwise specified, and 4 in. glass beaded fringe.

	Not Wired	Wired	Complete No Lamps
1 Lt. Elec.	$26.00	$27.50	$27.90
2 Lt. Elec.	26.25	28.00	28.80

Extra Lengthening, per stem, per foot
Not Wired..$0.50   Wired..$0.60

No. 10318—BRUSH BRASS
Length, 36 in.

Includes 14 in. bent art glass dome, color No. 98, unless otherwise specified, and 4 in. glass beaded fringe.

	Not Wired	Wired	Complete No Lamps
1 Lt. Elec.	$17.50	$18.50	$18.90
2 Lt. Elec.	17.75	19.00	19.80

Extra Lengthening, per foot
Not Wired..$0.60   Wired..$0.70

No. 10317—BRUSH BRASS
Length, 36 in.

Includes 12 in. art glass dome, color No. 99, unless otherwise specified, and 4 in. glass beaded fringe.

	Not Wired	Wired	Complete No Lamp
1 Lt. Elec.	$12.00	$12.75	$13.15

Extra Lengthening, per foot
Not Wired.........$0.60   Wired.........$0.70

No. 10319—BRUSH BRASS
Length, 36 in.

Includes 16 in. art glass dome, as shown, colors No. 98 in body, No. 41 in corners, unless otherwise specified, with 4 in. glass beaded fringe.

	Not Wired	Wired	Complete No Lamps
1 Lt. Elec.	$18.00	$19.00	$19.40
2 Lt. Elec.	18.25	19.50	20.30

Extra Lengthening, per foot
Not Wired.........$0.60   Wired.........$0.70

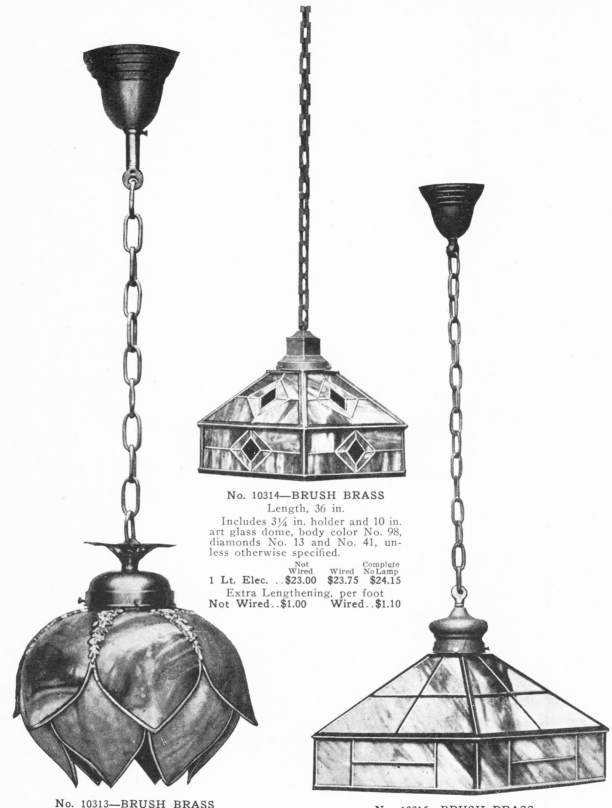

244

No. 10314—BRUSH BRASS

Length, 36 in.

Includes 3¼ in. holder and 10 in. art glass dome, body color No. 98, diamonds No. 13 and No. 41, unless otherwise specified.

	Not Wired	Wired	Complete No Lamp
1 Lt. Elec.	$23.00	$23.75	$24.15

Extra Lengthening, per foot

Not Wired..$1.00   Wired..$1.10

No. 10313—BRUSH BRASS

Length, 36 in.

Includes 12 in. tulip art glass shade, colors No. 98 and No. 12, as shown, in all prices.

	Not Wired	Wired	Complete No Lamp
1 Lt. Elec.	$20.00	$20.75	$21.15

Extra Lengthening, per foot

Not Wired.........$0.60   Wired.........$0.70

No. 10315—BRUSH BRASS

Length, 36 in.

Includes 14 in. art glass dome, color No. 98, unless otherwise specified.

	Not Wired	Wired	Complete No Lamp
1 Lt. Elec.	$18.00	$18.75	$19.15

Extra Lengthening, per foot

Not Wired.........$0.60   Wired.........$0.70

No. 10515—VERDE AN-TIQUE

Height, 24 in. Base, 7½ in.

Complete with 6 ft. silk lamp cord, pull chain sockets, and attachment plug.

3 Lt. Elec. $33.00

Diameter of dome, 18 in.

Colors of art glass, amber, green and ruby.

No. 10516—BRUSH BRASS

Height, 20½ in. Base, 8½ in.

Complete with 6 ft. silk lamp cord, pull chain sockets, and attachment plug.

3 Lt. Elec. $26.00

Diameter of dome, 15 in.

Colors of art glass, green.

No. 10520—VERDE AN-TIQUE

Height, 25 in. Base, 9 in.

Complete with 6 ft. lamp cord, pull chain sockets, and attachment plug.

3 Lt. Elec. $54.00

Diameter of dome, 18½ in.

Colors of art glass, amber, rose and green.

No. 10521—VERDE AN-TIQUE

Height, 25 in. Base, 9 in.

Complete with 6 ft. lamp cord, pull chain sockets, and attachment plug.

3 Lt. Elec. $46.00

Diameter of dome, 18 in.

Colors of art glass, green, amber and ruby.

No. 10513—VERDE AN-TIQUE

Height, 29 in. Base, 8½ in.

Complete with 6 ft. silk lamp cord, pull chain sockets, and attachment plug.

3 Lt. Elec. $90.00

Diameter of dome, 21 in.

Colors of glass, old rose, amber and green.

No. 10514—VERDE AN-TIQUE

Height, 25 in. Base, 9 in.

Complete with 6 ft. silk lamp cord, pull chain sockets, and attachment plug.

3 Lt. Elec. $48.00

Diameter of dome, 22 in.

Colors of art glass, amber, green and pearl.

No. 10517—BRUSH BRASS

Height, 23 in. Base, 8½ in.

Complete with 6 ft. silk lamp cord, pull chain sockets, and attachment plug.

2 Lt. Elec. $16.50

Diameter of dome, 16 in.

Colors of art glass, amber, old rose and green.

No. 10518—VERDE AN-TIQUE

Height, 27½ in. Base, 9 in.

Complete with 6 ft. silk lamp cord, pull chain sockets, and attachment plug.

3 Lt. Elec. $68.00

Diameter of dome, 20 in.

Colors of art glass, rose, pearl and green.

– Table lamps and hanging domes from the 1914 catalog of H. J. Peters Co., Chicago, Ill.

EXCLUSIVE LIGHTING EFFECTS **H.J. PETERS CO.** CHICAGO CREATORS CLASSIC DESIGNS

No. A996

No. A996—STOCK FINISH—BRUSHED BRASS AND BLACK.

Height 25 in. Shade 17½ in.

Art Glass Shade with Heavy Cast Over-Metal Scenic Design.

Wired
Complete as
shown except
Lamps

3-Lt. Elec. **$39.50**

Stock color, upper panels sunset art glass, water scene blue art glass.
Price includes pull chain sockets, 6 ft. silk cord and swivel attachment plug.

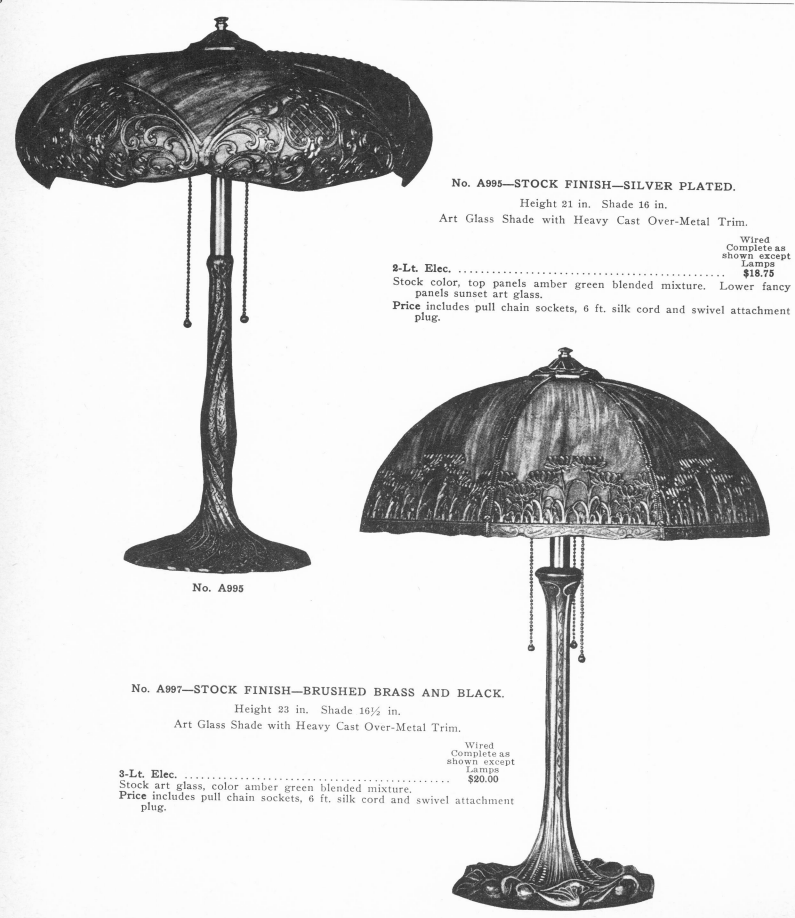

No. A995—STOCK FINISH—SILVER PLATED.

Height 21 in.   Shade 16 in.

Art Glass Shade with Heavy Cast Over-Metal Trim.

Wired
Complete as
shown except
Lamps

2-Lt. Elec. **$18.75**

Stock color, top panels amber green blended mixture. Lower fancy panels sunset art glass.

Price includes pull chain sockets, 6 ft. silk cord and swivel attachment plug.

No. A995

No. A997—STOCK FINISH—BRUSHED BRASS AND BLACK.

Height 23 in.   Shade 16½ in.

Art Glass Shade with Heavy Cast Over-Metal Trim.

Wired
Complete as
shown except
Lamps

3-Lt. Elec. **$20.00**

Stock art glass, color amber green blended mixture.

Price includes pull chain sockets, 6 ft. silk cord and swivel attachment plug.

No. A997

No. A993—STOCK FINISH—ANTIQUE BRUSHED BRASS.

Height 21 in.   Shade 15½ in.

Art Glass Shade with Heavy Cast Over-Metal Trim.

Wired
Complete
as shown
except
Lamps

2-Lt. Elec. **$21.50**

Stock color art glass amber top panels, water scene blue.

Price includes pull chain sockets, 6 ft. silk cord and swivel attachment plug.

No. A993

No. A992—STOCK FINISH—ANTIQUE BRUSHED BRASS.

Height 20½ in.   Shade 12 in.

Art Glass Shade with Heavy Cast Over-Metal Trim.

Wired
Complete
as shown
except
Lamps

2-Lt. Elec. **$19.50**

Stock color, amber art glass.

Price includes pull chain sockets, 6 ft. silk cord and swivel attachment plug.

No. A992

No. A3703 – Stock Finish – Brushed Brass.
Length 42 in.   Dome 24 in.
Bent Panel Dome in Solid Brass Frame with Heavy Cast Over-Metal
Trim.

	Not Wired	Wired	Complete as shown except Lamps
1-Lt. Elec.	32.20	33.20	33.88
2-Lt. Elec.	32.45	33.70	35.06
3-Lt. Elec.	32.70	34.20	36.24
4-Lt. Elec.	32.95	34.70	37.42

Includes 24 in. Art glass dome with fancy imported Wedding Bell fringe
    in all prices. Stock color, amber art glass.
Complete price includes pull chain sockets.
Extra lengthening No. 712 solid brass chain stem, per foot,
Not Wired .... 1.25   Wired 1.35

Hanging light fixtures from the 1914
catalog of the H. J. Peters Co., Chicago, Ill.

No. A3703

No. G266
Rich Amber Iri-
descent Lustre.
Each
2¼x6 In.....$3.50
2¼x7 In.....$4.00
Diameter of Shade
4¼ In.

No. G284
Rich Amber Iri-
descent Lustre.
Each
2¼x5 In.....$3.00
Diameter of Shade
4¼ In.

No. G267
Rich Amber Iri-
descent Lustre.
Each
2¼x5½ In....$4.00
Diameter of Shade
4½ In.

No. G350
Iridescent Pearl
Shell with Gold
and Green Lines.
Each
2¼x5¾ In...$3.00
Diam. of Shade 6 in.

No. G354
Iridescent Pearl
Shell with Rich
Golden Decoration.
Each
3¼x6½ in......$9.00
Diameter of Shade
5 in.

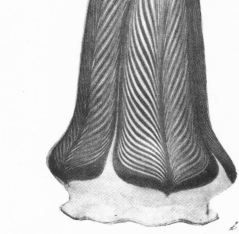

No. G355
Iridescent Pearl
Shell with Gold
and Green Lines.
Each
2¼x6½ in......$8.00
Diameter of Shade
4½ in.

— Table lamps and boudoir lamps from the Frankel Light Co., Cleveland, Ohio, catalog.

5905
Bronze Finish
Natural Vines and Leaves
Height, 28 in. over all
Base, 6¼ in. diameter
Wired complete with 6 ft. silk cord,
plug socket and
Yellow Frosted Grapes and Lamp

5901
Bronze Finish
Natural Vines and Leaves
Height, 27 in. over all
Base, 6¼ in. diameter
Wired with 6 ft. silk cord, plug
sockets, 2¼ in. electric holders,
Frosted Tulip Shades and Lamps

5902
Bronze Finish
Natural Vines and Leaves
Height, 27 in. over all
Base, 6¼ in. diameter
Wired with 6 ft. silk cord, plug
sockets, 2¼ in. electric holders
Frosted Tulip Shades and Lamps
2 lights

No. 214

Height 25 in.   Diam. of shade 18 in.
Electric wired with 2 pull chain sockets.
Gas—1 light complete.
Amber, amber-green, green, sunset glass.
Finishes: Stat. bronze, old gold, Dublin green.
List—Each $32.00

No. 216

Height 23 in.   Diam. of shade 16 in.
Electric wired with 2 pull chain sockets.
Amber, amber-green, green, sunset glass.
Finishes—Stat. bronze, old gold, Dublin green or Flemish.
List—Each $21.00

No. 220

Height 24½ in.   Diam. of shade 17 in.
Electric wired with 2 pull chain sockets.
Gas—1 light complete.
Finishes—Stat. bronze, old gold, Dublin green or Flemish.
List—Each $20.50

No. 212

Height 25 in.   Diam. of shade 18 in.
Electric wired with 2 pull chain sockets.
Gas—1 light complete.
Amber, amber-green, green, sunset glass.
Finishes: Stat. bronze, old gold, Dublin green.
List—Each $32.00

No. 253—Rec. D—2 Lights
Height 22½ in.   Width 16 in.
List $28.00

No. 253—Dec. C—2 Lights
Height 22½ in.   Width 16 in.
List $28.00

No. 215
Height 14 in.   Shade 7 in.
1 Light Electric Complete with Chain
Pull Socket
Silver. Ivory or Stat. Bronze…$11.00

No. 218—One Height
Height 15 in.   Width 8 in.
List $11.00

No. 219—One Height
Height 15 in.   Width 8 in.
List $3.50

No. 217—One Height
Height 15 in.   Width 8 in.
List $10.00

All Lamps in Assorted Finish

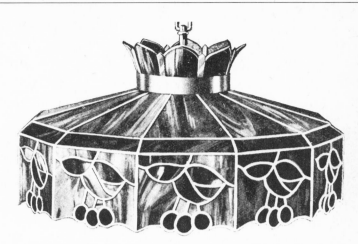

No. 7004. Diameter of dome 24 inches, $20.00. No charge for packing. $1.50 extra for stem or chain. We ship dome without stem or chain, except when specially ordered.

– Table lamps and hanging domes from a catalog published by the Cincinnati Artistic Wrought Iron Works, Cincinnati, Ohio.

No. 1042   **No. 1027-S**   **No. 1010-A.**

No. 1042. Height, 25 inches. Diameter of shade, 15 inches. Verde green finish. $14.50. **No. 1010-A.** Height, 26½ inches. Shade, 23 inches. $50.00. **No. 1027-S.** Height, 15½ inches. Shade, 8 inches. Swedish iron finish. $10.00.

No. 1010-C. Electric Lamp. Height to top 32 inches. Diameter of shade 22 inches. Verde green or brushed brass, $34.00. Fast seller, try a sample.

257

No. 627. Height, 27 inches. Dome, 15 inches. Art glass and fringe. Gas, $21.00. Same for electric complete, wired, $23.00. 25 per cent. extra for old copper.

No. 7005. Diameter of dome 24 inches. Brushed brass finish. No charge for packing, $26.00. Stem or chain $1.50. We ship dome without stem or chain except when ordered.

No. 7005-A. Same dome, only 20 inches. $20.00. These domes are fast sellers, try a sample.

No. 1010. Brushed brass. Height, 28 inches. Dome, 18 inches. 4 electric. $46.00.

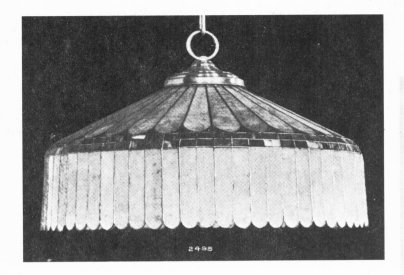

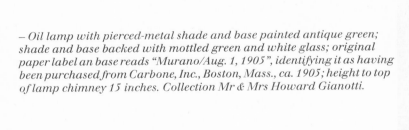

2495

– Oil lamp with pierced-metal shade and base painted antique green; shade and base backed with mottled green and white glass; original paper label an base reads "Murano/Aug. 1, 1905", identifying it as having been purchased from Carbone, Inc., Boston, Mass., ca. 1905; height to top of lamp chimney 15 inches. Collection Mr & Mrs Howard Gianotti.

275

1184

1183

PLATE 190

2109

2110

2466

2458

2478

2409

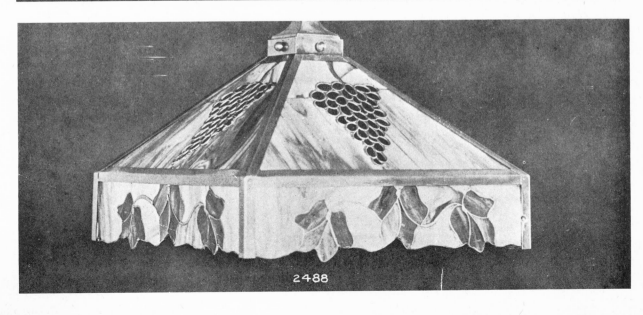

2488

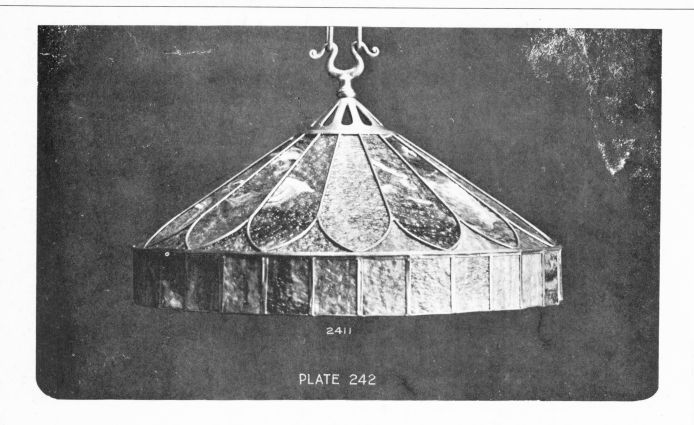

2411

PLATE 242

2491

2449

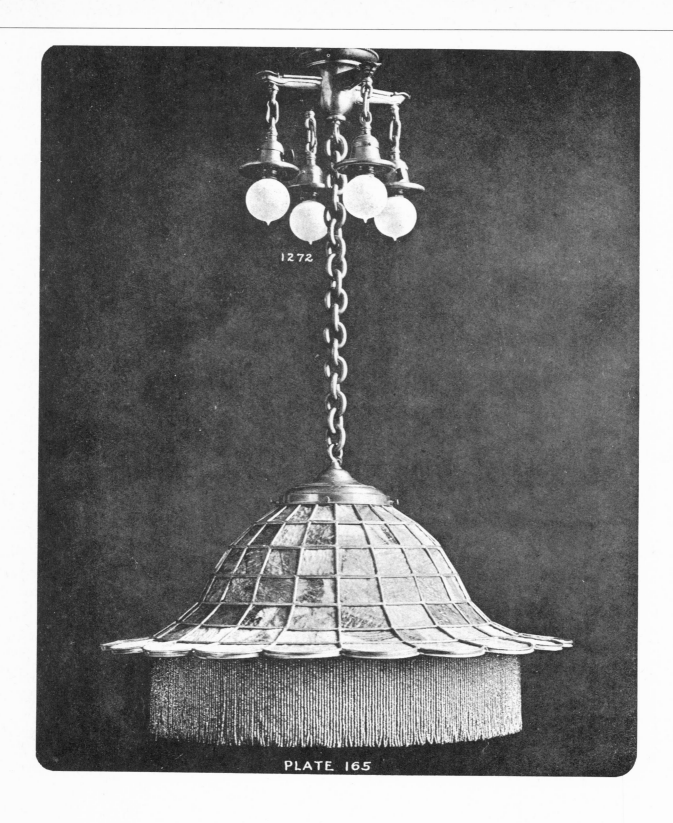

1272

PLATE 165

265

1168

1170

PLATE 167

— Table lamps and a ceiling fixture with bunches of grapes for shades;
from a catalog of The Albert Sechrist Manufacturing Co., Denver, Colo.

— Hanging lamp fixtures from a catalog of The Albert Sechrist Manufacturing Co., Denver, Colo.

2421

2425

2422

2424

2423

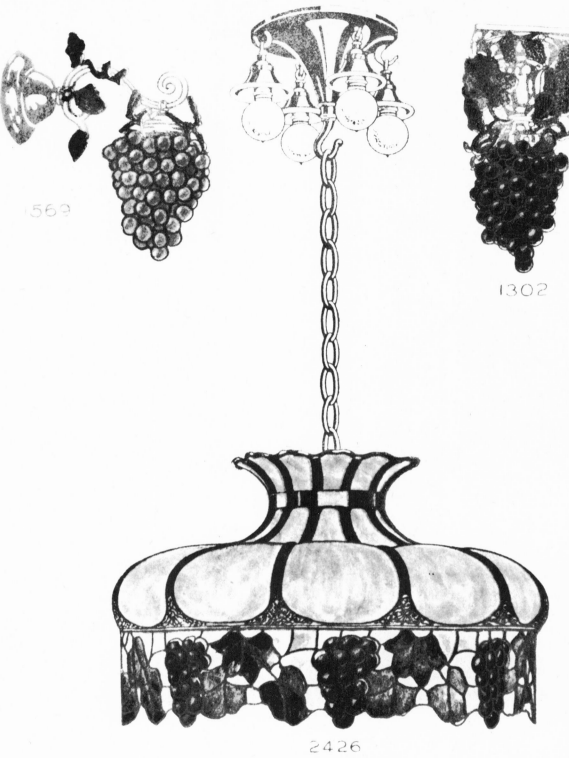

1569

1302

2426

2430

Art-glass and Bent-glass hanging domes and a lamp; from an original
catalog published by R. Williamson & Co., Chicago, Ill.

– Table lamps from a catalog of The Albert Sechrist Manufacturing Co., Denver, Colo.

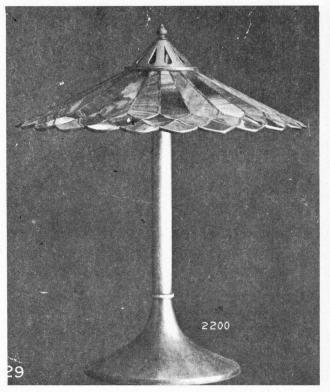

2200

29

TE 225

1194

2220

224

1193

2229

293

1199

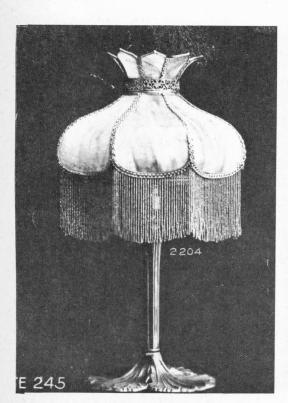

2204

E 245

2202

234

2235

Bibliography and Sources

Works of General Interest

Amaya, *Tiffany Glass*, New York 1967

Art Deco Style in Household Objects, Architecture, Sculpture, Graphics, Jewelry, New York 1972

Arwas, Victor, *Glass Art Nouveau to Art Deco*, London 1977

Aslin, Elizabeth, *The Aesthetic Movement*, London 1969

Bairati, Eleonora; Bossaglia, Rossana; Rosci, Marco, *L'Italia Liberty*, Milan 1973

Bajot, Emile, *L'Art Nouveau et Ameuble*, Paris 1898

Bangert, Albrecht, *Jugendstil*, Munich 1976

Barilli, Renato, *Il Liberty*, Milan 1966

Battersby, Martin, *Art Nouveau*, 1969

Battersby, Martin, *The Decorative Twenties*, London 1969

Battersby, Martin, *The Decorative Thirties*, London 1971

Bayer, Herbert and Gropius, Walter, *Bauhaus 1919-1928*, Stuttgart 1955

Belling, Helmut, *Jugendstil – Der Weg ins 20. Jahrhundert*, 1959

Bloch-Dermant, Janine, *L'Art du verre en France 1860-1914*, Freiburg 1974

Blount, *French Cameo Glass*, Iowa 1968

Brunhammer, Yvonne, *Le Style 1925*, Paris 1975

Brunhammer, Yvonne, *Art Nouveau Belgium France*, Chicago 1976

Brunhammer, Yvonne, *The Nineteen Twenties Style*, London 1969

Buffet-Challié, Laurence, *Le Modern Style*, Paris 1975

Clark, Robert Judson, *The Arts and Crafts Movement in America 1876-1916*, Princeton 1972

Cremona, I., *Die Zeit des Jugendstils*, Munich 1966

Dingelstedt, Kurt, *Jugendstil in der angewandten Kunst*, 1959

Eisler, Max, *Dagobert Peche*, Vienna – Leipzig 1925

Eisler, Max, *Österreichische Werkkultur*, Vienna 1916

Feuchtmüller, Rupert; Mrazek, Wilhelm, *Kunst in Österreich 1860-1918*, Vienna 1964

Fred, W., *Die Wohnung und ihre Ausstattung*, Bielefeld and Leipzig 1903

Garner, Philippe, *Emile Gallé*, London 1976

Günther, Sonja, *Interieurs um 1900*, Munich 1971

Hammacher, A. M., *Le Monde de Henry van de Velde*, Paris 1967

Heintschel, Hella, *Lampen, Leuchter, Laternen seit der Antike*, Innsbruck 1975

Hillier, Bevis, *Art Deco of the 20s and 30s*, London 1968

Hilschenz, H., *Das Glas des Jugendstils*, Kunstmuseum Düsseldorf, 1973

Hoeber, F., *Peter Behrens*, Munich 1913

Jahrbuch des deutschen Werkbundes, Jena 1910 ff

Jaeger, Carl and Fraunberger, Georg, *Kunstgläser*, Munich 1922

Janneau, Guillaume, *Le Luminaire* (2 Vols.), Paris 1925

Klamkin, Marian, *The Collector's Book of Art Nouveau*, 1971

Koch, R., *Louis Comfort Tiffany*, New York 1958

Koch, R., *Louis Comfort Tiffany's Glass, Bronzes, Lamps*, New York 1971

Koch, R., *Louis Comfort Tiffany – Rebel in Glass*, New York 1966

Koch, R., *Stained Glass Decades, A Study of L. C. Tiffany and the Art Nouveau in America*, Yale University 1957

Koreska-Hartmann, Linda, *Jugendstil – Stil der Jugend*, Munich 1969

Lanoux, Armand, *Paris 1925*, Cologne 1959

Loeb, Marcia, *Art Deco Designs and Motifs, 100 Examples*, New York 1972

Lugiano & Golson, *Stained Glass Lamp Art*, New York 1976

Maenz, Paul, *Art Deco 1920-1940*, Cologne 1974

McClinton, Katherine M., *Lalique for Collectors*, London 1975

McClinton, Katherine M., *Art Deco – Guide for Collectors*, New York 1972

Menten, Theodore, *The Art Deco Style*, New York 1972

Müller, Dr Hans, *Jugendstil*, Leipzig 1972

Neustadt, E., *The Lamps of Tiffany*, New York 1970

Neuwirth, W., *Das Glas des Jugendstils*, Österr. Museum für angewandte Kunst, Vienna 1973

Papini, Roberto, *Le arti d'oggi*, Milan 1930

Pazaurek, Gustav E., *Kunstgläser der Gegenwart*, Leipzig 1925

Pazaurek, Gustav E., *Moderne Gläser*, Leipzig 1901

Pélichet, Edgar, *La Céramique Art Nouveau*, Lausanne 1976

Petzet, H. W., *Heinrich Vogeler*, Cologne 1972

Quénioux, Gaston, *Les Arts décoratifs modernes*, Paris 1925

Revi, M., *American Art Nouveau Glass*, New York 1968

Rheims, M., *La Sculpture au XIXᵉ*, Paris 1972

Rheims, M., *Kunst um 1900*, 1965

Rheims, M., *The Flowering of Art Nouveau*, New York (no date)

Rheims, M., *L'Object 1900 – art et métiers graphiques*, 1964

Roberts, Darrah L., *Collecting Art Nouveau Shades*, Iowa 1972

Schmidt, L., *Jugendstil*, London 1972

Schmutzler, Robert, *Art Nouveau – Jugendstil*, Stuttgart 1962

Seling, Helmut, *Jugendstil*, Heidelberg/Munich 1959

Sembach, Klaus-Jürgen, *Stil 1930*, Tübingen 1971

Speenburgh, G., *The Arts of the Tiffanys*, Chicago 1956

Sterner, G., Dissertation "Die Vasen der Gebrüder Daum", Munich 1969

The Collector's Encyclopedia, London 1974

Tschudi-Madsen, Stefan, *Jugendstil, Europäische Kunst der Jahrhundertwende*, Munich 1967

Uecker, Wolf, *Art Déco*, Munich 1974

van de Velde, Henry, *Der neue Stil in Frankreich*, Berlin 1925

Veronesi, Giulia, *Style 1925*, Lausanne 1968

Vollmer, E., *Künstlerlexikon*, Leipzig (no date)

Waissenberger, Robert, *Die Wiener Secession*, Vienna 1971

Walters, Thomas, *Art Deco*, London 1973

Weatherman, Hazel Marie, *Colored Glassware of the Depression Era*, Missouri 1970

Wechssler-Kümmel, Sigrid, *Schöne Lampen, Leuchter und Laternen*, Heidelberg/Munich 1962

Werner, Bruno E., *Die Zwanziger Jahre*, Munich 1962

Wichmann, Siegfried, *Jugendstil*, Munich 1977

Index

Abbreviations

~	circa
Ø	Diameter
H	Height
Ill.	Illustration
L	Length
Lit.	Literature
Pl.	Plate
Sign.	Signed
W	Width